UNIX System Command Summary
for UNIX System V

by Specialized Systems
Consultants, Inc. (SSC)

This book is printed
on recycled paper.

UNIX is a registered trademark of Unix
Systems Laboratories

SSC is a registered tradename of Specialized
Systems Consultants, Inc.

PostScript is a registered trademark of Adobe
Systems, Inc.

PDP and VAX are registered trademarks of
Digital Equipment Corporation.

ED COMMANDS

Many commands are of the form *address command*. In these commands, the items in parentheses indicate default address values.

Two values separated by a comma indicate an address range.

re refers to a regular expression. (See Page 88.)

nre refers to a new (replacement) regular expression.

Addresses:

.	current line
$	last line
n	*n*th line
'*x*	line marked as *x* with **k** command
/*re*/	first line (forward) *re*
?*re*?	first line (backward) *re*

Commands (default addresses shown in ( )):

(.)**a**	append; end with period alone on a line
(.,.)**c**	change; end with period alone on a line
(.,.)**d**	delete lines
e [*file*]	edit *file*
E [*file*]	edit *file*; no diagnostics
f [*file*]	set current filename
(1,$)**g**/*re*/*cmds*	global on matching lines
(1,$)**G**/*re*/*cmds*	interactive global
h	explain last **?** diagnostic
H	toggle explanatory diagnostics mode
(.)**i**	insert; end with period alone on a line
(.,.+1)**j**	join lines
(**k**)*x*	set mark *x* at addressed line
(.,.)**l**	list displaying special characters
(.,.)**m***a*	move lines after line *a*
(.,.)**n**	print with line numbers
(.,.)**p**	print lines
P	toggle * prompt
q	quit
Q	quit, discarding any changes
($)**r** [*file*]	read *file*
(.,.)**s**/*re*/*nre*/	substitute *nre* for *re*
(.,.)**s**/*re*/*nre*/**g**	like above but all occurrences in line
(.,.)**s**/*re*/*nre*/*n*	match only *n*th occurrence of *re*
(.,.)**t***a*	copy lines after line *a*
u	undo previous substitution
(1,$)**v**/*re*/*cmds*	like **g** but unmatched lines
(1,$)**V**/*re*/*cmds*	like **G** but unmatched lines
(1,$)**w** [*file*]	write [to file]
X	encrypt during **e**, **r** or **x**
($) =	print line number
!*cmd*	execute *cmd* as UNIX command
(.+1)<nl>	print specified line

Note: If *file* (in **e**, **E** or **r**) begins with **!** it is a UNIX command whose output is input to the edit buffer. In **w**, !*file* uses buffer as input to command.

UNIX System Command Summary
for UNIX System V

This booklet is designed as a reference for the experienced UNIX user and as a learning tool for the newcomer. It is based on UNIX System V, Releases 2, 3 and 4. It includes commands accessible to the normal user; most maintenance, graphics, and superuser commands are not included.

Three special sections cover details of specific commands:

Usage Notes

Command names are organized alphabetically. Several conventions are used to concisely define commands.

User commands are flagged as follows:

Δ	Text processing and DWB commands
Θ	Development system commands

Each command description consists of a title line, one or more invocation lines and definitions of the fields within the command.

The title line describes the command. The invocation lines show the syntax of the command. If there are multiple ways to invoke the command, they are shown in multiple invocation lines. Within the invocation lines the following conventions are used:

- A % is used to represent the system prompt and is not typed by the user
- **Boldface** is used to represent items which must be typed exactly as shown
- *Italics* are used to represent items that are to be substituted for (such as filenames)
- Brackets [ ] surround items that are optional; do not type the brackets (unless otherwise specified)

The following special abbreviations are used to minimize redundant text:

- **stdin** represents the standard input: by default, this is the terminal keyboard
- **stdout** represents the standard output: by default this is the terminal screen
- **stderr** represents the standard error: by default, this is the terminal screen
- *option* represents the selection of an option from the list following the command line
- *file* represents a file name
- *arg* represents an argument
- Plurals (i.e., *options*, *files*, or *args*) imply that multiple occurrences are permitted
- Numbered arguments (e.g., *file1*, *file2*) indicate a precise number of occurrences is required
- Options that take arguments generally need to be entered separately from other options with their arguments immediately following

Usage Notes, continued

For the shell to parse a command line correctly, the arguments must be separated by whitespace or punctuation. Whitespace consists of one or more space characters, tab characters and/or the end of line character.

In many commands, use of spaces between option letters and the following words is optional. For example, both **– o** *file* and **– o***file* may be valid.

Many commands accept – – as an optional flag to indicate the end of the option list. This is useful where a file name begins with a dash.

In some cases, it may be necessary to quote arguments to commands in order to protect special characters from interpretation by the shell. See the shell section of this Command Summary or the SSC Pocket Tutorial on the shell for more information.

Disclaimer and Bug Reports.

Some options and commands are specific to a release and implementation. In addition, these systems run on many different platforms, and your system may deviate from the commands and options in this book.

Mail bug reports to SSC (see Page 1 for address) or send them electronically to **products@ssc.com**.

300, 300S — DASI 300, 300s Terminal Handler
% **300** [*options*]
% **300s** [*options*]
Options:
    + 12   set 12 pitch, 6 lpi
    – d*t,l,c*   insert null after t tabs, c chars; insert 20 nulls
                  if line length > l (**– d3,90,30** default)
    – n n is 1/48 inch increments for 1/2 line feed
                  (**4** default)

4014 — Tektronix 4014 Paginator
% **4014** [*options*] [*file*]
Options:
    – c*n* n column output, wait after last column
    – n   no erase before print
    – p*l*   page length to l, scale: **inches, lines**
    – t   no wait betweeb pages

450 — DASI 450 Terminal Handler
% **450**

ACCTCOM — Process Accounting
% **acctcom** [*options*] [*files*]
    stdin read if no *files* specified and **stdin** is not
    a terminal or **/dev/null**, else **/var/adm/pacct** read
Options:
    – a   also print average statistics
    – b   read backwards, most recent commands first
    – C *n*   only processes with CPU time > n seconds
    – d *mm/dd* only processes for specified day
    – e *time*   only processes existing at or before *time*
    – E *time*   only processes ending at or before *time*
    – f   print **fork/exec** flag and exit status
    – g *group* only processes of *group* (group *ID* or *name*)
    – h   print "hog factor," (CPU/elapsed time)
    – H *factor* only processes exceeding "hog factor"
    – i   print I/O counts
    – I *chars* only processes transferring > *chars*
    – k   print kcore-minutes
    – l *line*   only processes on **/dev/term/***line*
    – m   print mean core size (default)
    – n *pat*   only commands matching pattern *pat*
    – o *output* put records in *output*, not on **stdout**
    – O *n*   only processes with sys CPU > n seconds
    – q   only print average statistics
    – r   print "CPU factor," (user/(sys+user) time)
    – s *time*   only processes existing at or after *time*
    – S *time*   only processes starting at or after *time*
    – t   separate user and system CPU times
    – u *user* only processes of *user* (*user-ID*, *login-name*,
                  # (superuser), ? (unknown user-ID))
    – v   don't print column headings

    time   *hr* [:*min* [:*sec*]]

Θ **ADB** — General Purpose Debugger
% **adb** [*option*] [*objfile* [*corefile*]]
Options:
    – w   open both *objfile* and *corefile* for update

Arguments:
    objfile   executable file (**a.out** default)
    corefile   core image dump file (**core** default)

5

(continued)

Request format:

    [*address*] [,*count*] [*command*][;]
    address and *count* are expressions
    address   set . to *address* (**0** default)
    count   **1** default

Command Format: *verb* [*modifiers*]

Verbs:

<newline>
           repeat previous command with *count* = **1**
?*fmt*   print from *address* in *objfile* in specified *fmt*
/*fmt*   print from *address* in *corefile* in specified *fmt*
=*fmt*   print value of *address* in specified *fmt*
[?/]l *val mask*
           search for *val* after and with *mask* (**1** default)
[?/] L *val mask*   as above but 4 bytes instead of 2
[?/] m *b1 e1 f1* **[?/]** set new map values
[?/] w *values*   write 2-byte *value* to current location
[?/] W *values*   write 4-byte *value* to current location
>*name*   assign value of . to *name*
!*cmd*   call new shell to execute *cmd*

Modifiers:

$<*file*   switch command input to *file*
$>*file*   append output to *file*
$a   ALGOL 68 stack backtrace
$b   print all breakpoints
$c   print C backtrace (*count* specifies levels)
$C   same as **$c**, plus variables
$d   set radix to *address*
$e   print external variable values and names
$f   print floating point registers in single or
           double length
$m   print address map
$o   set integer input to octal
$q   exit from **adb**
$r   print registers and set . to **pc**
$s   set symbol match limit to address
           (**255** default)
$v   print non-zero variables in octal
$w   set page width (**80** default)
:b*cmd*   set breakpoint, execute *cmd* when
           encountered
:c*signal*   continue process sending it *signal*
:d   delete breakpoint at *address*
:k   kill current subprocess
:r   run *objfile* as subprocess, *count* specifies
           number of breakpoints to ignore
:s*signal*   like **c** but single step *count* times

Θ **ADMIN** — Administer SCCS Files

% **admin** [*options*] *files*

    files either begin with **s.** or are directories
    names of SCCS files read from **stdin** if *files* is −

Options:

    − **a***user*   authorize *user* to make **deltas**
    − **d***flag*[*val*] delete specified flag (see − **f**)
    − **e***user*   erase *user*'s **delta** authorization

(continued)

– **f***flag*[*val*]	set flags with optional values:	
	b	permit branch deltas
	c*high*	set highest release (**9999** default)
	d*n*	set **get**'s default delta number
	f*low*	set lowest release (**1** default)
	i[*str*]	fatal error if no ID keywords or no keywords matching optional *str*
	j	permit multiple **get**s at once
	l*list*	lock releases not to be edited
	m*text*	*text* replaces ID keyword **%M%**
	n	make null deltas for skipped releases
	q*text*	*text* replaces ID keyword **%Q%**
	t*text*	*text* replaces ID keyword **%Y%**
	v[*file*]	**delta**s request Modification Request numbers, *file* is a checking program
– **h**	verify file integrity via SCCS checksum	
– **i**[*file*]	source for new file (**stdin** default) (implies – **n**), only one – **i** per **admin** command	
– **m**[*list*]	*list* of Modification Numbers inserted as reason for first delta	
– **n**	create new SCCS file, file empty if no – **i**	
– **r***n*	set initial release delta number to *n*	
– **t**[*file*]	source of descriptive text (required with – **i** and – **n**); if no *file*, descriptive text removed	
– **y**[*text*]	*text* is comment for initial delta valid only with – **i** or – **n**	
– **z**	"correct" checksum ignoring file corruption	

Θ **AR** — Maintain Archives and Libraries
% **ar** [–**V**] – *key afile files*

– **V**	print version information

key is one character from the set **dmpqrtx** and optionally one or more from **abcilsuv**

c	create *afile* without message
d	delete *files* from *afile*
l	place temporary files in local directory (/**tmp** default)
m[*pc posname*]	
	move *files* to specified place (end of file default)
p	print *files* in *afile*
q	quickly append *files* to end of *afile*
r[*option*][*pc posname*]	
	replace *files*
	u update only if newer
s	create symbol table
t	print table of contents of *afile* (all *files* default)
v[*option*]	verbose
	p precede each *file* printed with name
	t long listing of file information
x	extract *files*
pc	positioning character (used with **r** or **m**)
	a after *posname*
	b before *posname*
	i before *posname*
posname	name of file in the archive, used to specify where to move files
afile	name of archive or library

Θ **ARCV** — Convert Archive File Format
% **arcv** *in out*
   update archive files from PDP-11 to System V format

Θ **AS** — Assembler
% **as** [*options*] *files*
Options:
–dl	don't produce line no. info in object file
–j	use 'long'jump'assembler (VAX only)
–m	run input through **m4** preprocessor
–n	turn off long/short address optimization
–o *output*	name of output file (*file*.**o** default)
–Qn	suppress tool ID information (default)
–Qy	put tool ID information in output
–R	delete *file* after assembly
–T	accept obsolete assembler directives
–V	print version information
–Y[*i*],*dir*	look in *dir* for:
d	predefined macros
m	**m4** preprocessor

Θ **ASA** — Interpret Fortran ASA Carriage Controls
% **asa** [*files*]
   stdin read if no *files* specified

AT — Execute Commands Later
% **at** [*options*] *time* [*day*] [+*n unit*]
   add queue entry
Options:
–f *script*	read commands from *script*
–m	send mail to user after completion
time	1-4 digits and optional **am**, **pm**, **zulu** (GMT) or **noon**, **midnight**, **now**, or **next**
day	month name followed by date, day of week, **today** or **tomorrow** (some abbreviations accepted)
n unit	*n* **minutes**, **hours**, **days**, **weeks**, **months**, or **years**

% **at** [*option*]   check queue status
Options:
–l [*jobs*]	display job numbers of submitted jobs
–r *jobs*	remove jobs scheduled by **at** or **batch**

ATQ — Display "at" Queue in Execution Order
% **atq** [*option*] [*usernames*]
Options:
–c	display in order submitted
–n	display only number of jobs in queue

ATRM — Remove Jobs From "at" Queue
% **atrm** [*option*] [*args*]
Options:
–a	all jobs for current user
–f	suppress removal information (force)
–i	prompt to verify before removal (interactive)

args can be user names and/or job numbers

AWK — Pattern Scanning Language (See Page 80)
% **awk** [*options*] [*prog*] [*params*] [*files*]
    stdin read if − or no *files* specified
Options:
    −f *pfile*   use *pfile* as program
    −Fc   field separator character is *c*

prog   program line (should be in single quotes)
params   form **x**=..., **y**=...

BANNER — Print Banner with Large Letters
% **banner** *string*

string   10 characters maximum

BASENAME — Delete Prefix and Suffix from Pathname
% **basename** *string* [*suffix*]

string   pathname to filter
suffix   optional suffix to delete

BATCH — Run Command When System Load Permits
% **batch**
    stdin queued as background job

BC — Unlimited Precision Arithmetic Language
% **bc** [*option*] [*files*]
    stdin read after all *files*
Options:
    −c   compile only
    −l *lib*   math library (**sin, exp, log, arctan, Bessel**)

BDIFF — Compare Big Files
% **bdiff** *file1 file2* [*options*]
    stdin read if − specified for *file1* or *file2*
Options:
    n   set size of split segments to *n* (**3500** default)
    −s   suppress diagnostics

BFS — Big File Scanner (Read-Only **ed**)
% **bfs** [*option*] *file*
Option:
    −   suppress printing of *file* size

Θ **BS** — Compiled/Interpreted Language
% **bs** [*file* [*args*]]

file   read before **stdin**
args   passed to program

CAL — Print Calendar
% **cal** [[*month*] *year*]

month   number between 1 and 12 (current month default)
year   number between 1 and 9999 (full year default)

CALENDAR — Reminder Service
% **calendar** [*option*]
Option:
–	check everyone's **calendar** file and mail items for today and tomorrow

CANCEL — Cancel Printer Requests Made By **lp**
% **cancel** [*IDs*] [*printer*]
% **cancel –u** *user* [*printer*]

CAT — Concatenate and Print Files
% **cat** [*options*] [*files*]
    stdin read if – or no *files* specified
Options:
–e	with **–v** shows **$** before each newline
–s	silent about nonexistent files
–t	with **–v** shows tabs as ˆI and formfeeds as ˆL
–u	unbuffered output
–v	show non-printing characters (except tabs, newlines and formfeeds)

Θ **CB** — Beautify C Programs
% **cb** [*options*] [*files*]
    stdin read if no *files* specified
Options:
–j	join split lines
–l *n*	split lines longer than *n* characters
–s	use style specified in Kernighan and Ritchie
–V	print version information

Θ **CC** — C Compiler
% **cc** [*options*] *files*
    unrecognized options are passed to **ld**
Options:
–A *name* [(*def*)]	associate *name* with *def* as if by **#assert**
–A –	forget predefined macros and assertions
–B dynamic	link with **lib**x**.so** first
–B static	link with **lib**x**.a**
–b *string*	substitute compiler passes
–c	suppress link edit; produce **.o** files
–C	preprocessor does not delete comments
–dl	don't generate line no. info for symbolic debugger
–dn	static linking
–ds	don't generate symbol info for symbolic debugger
–dsl	combine **–dl** and **–ds** (default)
–dy	dynamic linking (default)
–D *name*[=*def*]	define *name* as *def* (**1** default)
–E	only preprocessor output to **stdout**
–f	use floating point software
–F	generate code for single-precision arithmetic
–g	generate **sdb** debugger info
–G	produce shared object instead of dynamic link
–H	print pathname of each included file on **stderr**
–I *dir*	search for files in *dir* before standard

(continued)

CC, continued
    – Jsfm   use assembly language math lib (**libsfm.sa**)
    – K[*mode,goal*,**PIC**,**minabi**]
                 (options can appear in comma-delimited list)
        mode   **fpe** software floating point
                 mau hardware math accelerator
        goal   **sd** optimize for speed
                 sz optimize size
                 – O must be specified with **sd** or **sz**
     PIC   generate position-independent code
     minabi   minimize dynamic linking
    – l *x*   search **libx.so** or **libx.a**
    – L *dir*   prepend *dir* to library search list
    – o *output* name of output file (**a.out** default)
    – O   optimize object code produced
    – p   set up object files for profiling
    – P   only preprocessor output to *files*.**i**
    – q l   invoke basic block analyzer
    – q p   set up object files for profiling (same as **– p**)
    – Q n   suppress tool ID information
    – Q y   put tool ID information in output (default)
    – S   put assembler source in *files*.**s** only
    – t[*passes*] indicate which passes to substitute
    – U *symb*   remove initial definition of *symb*
    – v   perform strict semantic checks
    – V   print version information
    – W *pass, arg1*[,*args*]
                 give arguments to *pass*
                 args is a comma-separated list
                 pass   one or more of **p02bal**
                      p   preprocessor
                      0   compiler
                      2   optimizer
                      b   basic block analyzer
                      a   assembler
                      l   link editor
    –X a   ANSI conformance but warn about
                 promotion rule changes
    –X c   conformance – full ANSI (**_ _STDC_ _**
                 set to 1)
    –X t   transition – accept compatible pre-ANSI code
    – Y *item,dir*
                 item can be any *tool* from **–W** option or
                 special characteristic specified below:
                      I   add last include directory
                      P   replace **ld** libraries
                          (comma-separated list)
                      S   directory containing start-up files

CD — Change Directory
% **cd** [*directory*]
    Environment variable **$HOME** used if no *directory*

Θ **CDC** — Change SCCS Delta Comments
% **cdc** [*options*] *files*
    SCCS filenames read from **stdin** if *files* is –
Options:
    – m*list*   add Modification Request numbers, remove
                 any preceded with an exclamation mark (**!**)
    – r*sid*   specify SCCS ID of delta to change
    – y[*text*]   replace comment with *text*

11

Θ **CFLOW** — Build External Reference Graph
% **cflow** [*options*] *files*
Options:
    – **A**name[(*def*)]
            associate *name* with *def* as if by **#assert**
    – **A** –   forget predefined macros and assertions
    – **d**n   cut off flow graph at depth *n*
    – **D**name[=*def*]
            define *name* as *def* (**1** default)
    – **i**_   include names starting with _
    – **ix**   include static data and external symbols
            (functions only default)
    – **I**dir   search for **.h** files in *dir* before standard
    – **r**   produce inverted listing
    – **U**symb   remove initial definition of *symb*

Δ **CHECKCW** — Check Constant Width Text (See **CW**)
% **checkcw** [*options*] *files*
Options:
    – **l**xx   define 1- or 2-character left delimiter
    – **r**xx   define 1- or 2-character right delimiter

Δ **CHECKEQ** — Check **eqn** Input (See **EQN**)
% **checkeq** [*files*]
    stdin read if no *files* specified

Δ **CHECKMM** — Check **mm** Macro Input (See **MM**)
% **checkmm** [*files*]
    stdin read if no *files* specified

CHGRP — Change Group ID of Files (See **CHOWN**)
% **chgrp** [*options*] *group files*
Options:
    – **h**   change group of symbolic link (not file)
    – **R**   recursive through subdirectories

group group name or decimal group-ID

CHMOD — Change Access Modes
% **chmod** [*option*] *mode files*
Option:
    – **R**   recursively descend through directories

mode can be numeric or symbolic. The symbolic case
consists of the form [**agou**][**+ – =**][**lrstwx**] where:

a	group, other and user access permissions (default)
g	group access permissions
o	other access permissions
u	user access permissions
+	add the permission to status of *files*
–	remove the permission from status of *files*
=	set the permission of *files* to specified value
l	mandatory locking
r	read permission
s	set owner ID or group ID on execution
t	save text mode; file owner only delete for directories
w	write permission
x	execute permission

g, **o** or **u** after the **=** uses the **g**roup, **o**ther or **u**ser
permission as a model
Multiple symbolic modes are separated by commas.

12

CHMOD, continued
The numeric case is formed from:

4000	set user ID on execution
20X**0**	set group ID on execution if X is **7**, **5**, **3**, **1**
	set mandatory locking if X is **6**, **4**, **2**, **0**
	(use symbolic mode to set or clear if *file* is
	directory)
1000	save text image after execution
	(sticky bit)
0X**00**	owner's permission, where X is OR of:
	4 (read), 2 (write), 1 (execute)
00X**0**	group's permission
000X	other's permission

CHOWN — Change Owner of Files
% **chown** [*options*] *owner files*
Options:

−h	change owner of symbolic link (not file)
−R	recursive through subdirectories

owner   login name or decimal user ID

CLEAR — Clear Terminal Screen
% **clear**

CMP — Compare Two Files
% **cmp** [*options*] *file1 file2*
   stdin read if − specified for *file1*
Options:

−l	print byte number and bytes
−s	silent, return exit codes only

Θ **COF2ELF** — COFF to ELF Object File Translation
% **cof2elf** [*options*] *files*
Options:

−i	continue translation on error
−q	quiet / suppress messages
−Qn	no ID information in output (default)
−Qy	put ID information in output
−s*dir*	save input files in *dir*
−V	print version information

Δ **COL** — Filter Reverse Line-Feeds from **stdin**
% **col** [*options*]
Options:

−b	printer cannot backspace
−f	forward half linefeed okay
−p	don't ignore unknown ESC sequences
−x	don't convert whitespace to tabs

Θ **COMB** — Combine SCCS Deltas
% **comb** [*options*] *files*
   SCCS filenames read from **stdin** if *files* is −
Options:

−c*list*	*list* of deltas to be preserved
−o	access as created file instead of most recent
−p*sid*	specify oldest delta to be preserved
−s	generate shell script to produce usage report

COMM — Select or Reject Common Lines
% comm [– *options*] *file1 file2*
    stdin read if – specified for *file1* or *file2*
Options:
1	suppress lines only from *file1*
2	suppress lines only from *file2*
3	suppress lines in both *file1* and *file2*

COMPRESS — Compress Files
% compress [*options*] *files*
    stdin read if – specified for *file1* or *file2*
Options:
– b *bits*	upper limit of common substring codes (9 to 16; 16 default)
– c	write to **stdout** instead of *file*.**Z**
– f	force compression (no prompts)
– v	display compression percentage

Θ **CONV** — Convert Common Object Files
% convert [*option*] *files*
    filenames read from **stdin** if – specified for files
Options:
– a	convert *files* to System V, release 2 portable archive format
– o	convert to pre-UNIX System V archive format
– p	convert to UNIX System 1.0 random access archive format
– t *target*	convert to byte ordering of *target* machine
target	**pdp**, **vax**, **ibm**, **x86**, **b16**, **n3b**, **mc68**, **m32** ok

Θ **CONVERT** — Format Archive and Object Files
% convert [*option*] *in out*
Option:
– 5	like Release 1.0
in	with **– 5** option: pre-UNIX System V Release 0 object file, link-edited module, archive of object files or a.out modules (VAX or 3B20 only) without **– 5** option: System V, Release 0 archive file (VAX or 3b20) or System V, Release 1.0 archive file
out	with **– 5** option: equivalent UNIX System V, release 1.0 file without **– 5** option: equivalent UNIX System V, release 2.0 file

CP — Copy Files
% cp [*options*] *file1 file2*
    make a copy of *file1* named *file2*
% cp *files directory*
    make copies of specified *files* in *directory*
Options:
– –	signifies end of options (optional)
– i	prompt before overwriting target
– p	preserve permissions and modification time
– r	recursively copy files and subdirectories

CPIO — Copy Archives
% **cpio – i[6bBcCdEfHIkmMrRsStTuvV]** [*patterns*]
    copy in: read **stdin**, select using *patterns*
% **cpio – o[aABcLTvV] –[CHMO]**
    copy out: pathnames from **stdin** to **stdout**
% **cpio – p[adlLmuvV]** *dir*
    copy out and in: read **stdin**, copy to directory *dir*
Options:

– 6	UNIX 6th edition format
– a	reset access times of input files after copy
– A	append to archive specified with **– O**
– b	swap bytes within each word
– B	5,120 bytes/record (for **/dev/rmt**? only)
– c	write header info as ASCII characters
– C *size*	block to *size* bytes/record
– d	create directories as needed
– E *file*	*file* contains list of filenames to extract
– f	copy all files not in *patterns*
– H *hdr*	read or write header in specified format **crc** or **CRC** ASCII w/expanded device numbers, **ustar** or **USTAR** IEEE/P1003 standard, **tar** or **TAR** **tar** format or **odc** ASCII w/small device numbers
– I *file*	read *file* as input archive
– k	skip corrupted headers
– l	link rather than copy whenever possible
– L	follow symbolic links
– m	retain previous file modification time
– M *message*	message for media switch (**%d** can be used for sequence number)
– O *file*	direct output to *file*
– r	rename files interactively
– R *ID*	assign owner and group info for files (super-user only)
– s	swap bytes
– S	swap halfwords
– t	print table of contents only
– T	truncate filenames > 14 characters
– u	copy disregarding age of files
– v	verbose, list filenames
– V	print dot for each file read/written

patterns	names of files to select, specified in shell notation (***** default)
dir	destination pathnames relative to this *dir*

Θ **CPP** — C Preprocessor
% **/lib/cpp** [*options*] [*input* [*output*]]
Options:

– C	pass comments (strip C-style comments default)
– D *name[=def]*	define *name* as *def* (**1** default)
– H	print included files on **stderr**
– I *dir*	search *dir* before standard ones
– P	don't produce line control info for C compiler
– T	include only first 8 characters to distinguish symbols
– U *symb*	remove initial definition of *symb*
– Y *dir*	search *dir* instead of standard

(continued)

CPP, continued

input	input for preprocessor (**stdin** default)
output	output of preprocessor (**stdout** default)
symb	reserved symbols include **ibm**, **gcos**, **tss**, **unix**, **interdata**, **pdp11**, **u370**, **u3b**, **vax**, **RES**, **RT**

Θ **CPRS** — Compress Common Object File
% **cprs** [*option*] *file1 file2*

    -p   print statistics

CRONTAB — Manipulate Crontab File
% **crontab** [*file*]

    stdin read if no *file* specified
% **crontab** [*option* [**-u** *user*]]
Options:

-e	edit or create empty file
-l	list user's crontab file
-r	remove user's crontab file from **/usr/spool/cron**

CRYPT — Encrypt/Decrypt **stdin** to **stdout**
% **crypt** [*password*]

    password is the key; if not given it is prompted for
% **crypt** [**-k**]

    use value of env variable **CRYPTKEY** as key

Θ **CSCOPE** — Interactively Examine C Program
% **cscope** [*options*] *files*
Options:

-b	build cross-reference only
-c	do not compress data
-C	ignore case when searching
-d	don't update cross reference
-e	suppress ^e prompt between files
-f *file*	use *file* instead of **cscope.out**
-i *file*	use *file* as list of source filenames
-I *dir*	search *dir* for include files
-l	enter line-oriented mode
-L	single search; used with **-n**
-n *pat*	go to input field *n* (0 is first) and search for *pat*
-p *n*	display last *n* components of path (**1** default)
-P *path*	prepend *path* to relative pathnames
-s *dir*	look in *dir* for sources
-T	use only 8 characters in symbol match
-u	unconditionally build cross-reference
-U	don't check file timestamps
-V	print version information

CSH — Invoke Shell With C-like Syntax
% **csh** [*options*] [*args*]
Options:

-b	force break in option processing
-c	read commands from first *arg*
-e	exit if command fails or non-zero exit status
-f	do not execute **.cshrc**; speeds start of shell
-i	force interactive mode
-n	parse commands without executing them
-s	commands read from **stdin**
-t	execute one command line, then exit

(continued)

CSH, continued
– v	print input lines as read
– V	like **– v**, except does it before reading **.cshrc**
– x	print commands as executed, with arguments
– X	like **– x**, except does it before reading **.cshrc**

CSPLIT — Split File
% **csplit** [*options*] *file args*
Options:
– f *prefix*	name new files *prefix***00** ... *prefixn* (**xx00** ... **xx***n* default)
– k	leave created files if error
– s	suppress character counts

args	where to split *file*, of the form:
/expr/	create file from current line up to line containing *expr*. May be followed by ±*n*.
%*expr***%**	same as */expr/*, no file creation
line	create file from current line to *line*
{*n*}	repeat previous argument *n* times

CT — Call Terminal and Start Login Process
% **ct** [*options*] *telnos*
Options:
– h	inhibit hangup
– s *speed*	set baud rate (**1200** default)
– v	send status information to **stderr**
– w*n*	wait up to *n* minutes for line
– x*n*	set debugging level to *n* (**0** to **9**)

telnos	list of phone numbers to try

CTAGS — Create a Tags File of Functions and Typedefs
% **ctags** [*options*] *sourcefiles*
Options:
– a	append output to existing tags file
– B	use backward searching pattern (?...?)
– f *file*	put tag descriptions in *file* (**tags** default)
– F	use forward searching pattern (/.../)
– t	create tags for typedefs
– u	update specified files in tags file
– v	produce function index on **stdout**
– w	suppress warnings
– x	print index of object names, line number, file name, and line text on **stdout**

Θ **CTRACE** — C Program Debugger
% **ctrace** [*options*] [*file*]
Options:
– A*name* [(*def*)]	associate *name* with *def* as if by **#assert**
– A–	forget predefined macros and assertions
– b	use only basic functions in trace code
– D *name*[=*def*]	define *name* as *def* (**1** default) (with **– P**)
– e	print variables in floating point also
– f *functions*	trace only *functions*
– I *dir*	search for **.h** files in *dir* before standard ones (with **– P**)

(continued)

CTRACE, continued

$-\mathbf{l}n$	check for looping trace output in n consecutively executed statements (**20** default, **0**=all)
$-\mathbf{o}$	print variables in octal also
$-\mathbf{p}$ *string*	change trace print function to *string* (**printf(** default)
$-\mathbf{P}$	preprocess before tracing input
$-\mathbf{Qn}$	don't add ID information to output (default)
$-\mathbf{Qy}$	add ID information to output
$-\mathbf{r}$ *file*	use *file* in place of **runtime.c**
$-\mathbf{s}$	suppress trace output from assignments and string copies
$-\mathbf{t}n$	trace n variables per statement (**10** default, **20** max)
$-\mathbf{u}$	print variables in unsigned format also
$-\mathbf{U}$ *symb*	remove definition of *symb* (with $-\mathbf{P}$)
$-\mathbf{v}$ *functions*	trace all but *functions*
$-\mathbf{V}$	print version information
$-\mathbf{x}$	print variables in hexadecimal also

file   contains C program to debug

CU — Call UNIX System
% **cu** [*options*] *destination*
Options:

$-\mathbf{b}n$	set character size to n bits (default is same as local terminal)
$-\mathbf{c}$*type*	use only device matching *type*
$-\mathbf{d}$	print diagnostic traces
$-\mathbf{e}$	set even parity
$-\mathbf{h}$	simulate half duplex terminal
$-\mathbf{l}$*line*	line device name (default is first available)
$-\mathbf{m}$	specify direct line with modem control
$-\mathbf{n}$	prompt for telephone number
$-\mathbf{o}$	set odd parity
$-\mathbf{s}$*speed*	set baud rate (**any** default)
$-\mathbf{t}$	set up auto-answer ASCII terminal

destination   phone number, system name or LAN address

enter ˜? to display the tilde command summary
enter ˜. to exit **cu**

Δ **CUT** — Cut Out Fields of File
% **cut** $-\mathbf{c}$*list* [*files*]
% **cut** $-\mathbf{f}$*list* [$-\mathbf{d}$*char*] [$-\mathbf{s}$] [*files*]
     stdin read if no *files* specified
Options:

$-\mathbf{c}$*list*	pass specified character positions
$-\mathbf{d}$*c*	specify field delimiter (**tab** default)
$-\mathbf{f}$*list*	pass specified fields
$-\mathbf{s}$	suppress lines with no delimiters
list	comma-separated list with optional − to indicate a range

Δ **CW** — Prepare Constant Width Text for Typesetting
% **cw** [*options*] [*files*]
    stdin read if no *files* specified
Options:
– **d**	print option settings on **stderr**
– **f***n*	position for constant width font (**3** default)
– **l***xx*	define 1- or 2-character left delimiter
– **r***xx*	define 1- or 2-character right delimeter
– **t**	transparent mode off
+ **t**	transparent mode on

Θ **CXREF** — Produce C Cross-Reference
% **cxref** [*options*] *files*
Options:
– **A***name* [(**def**)]	associate *name* with *def* as if by **#assert**
– **A**–	forget predefined macros and assertions
– **c**	print combined cross-reference
– **C**	run only first pass (create **.cx** file)
– **d**	disable printing declarations
– **D** *name* [=*def*]	define *name* as *def* (**1** default)
– **F**	print full path of referenced files
– **I** *dir*	search *dir* before standard ones
– **l**	don't print local variables
– **L** *n*	print in *n* columns (**5** default)
– **o** *output*	name of output file
– **s**	silent, don't print input filenames
– **t**	format output in columns of width 80
– **U** *symb*	remove definition of *symb*
– **V**	print version information
– **w** *n*	set width of output to *n* (**80** default)
– **W** *name,file,function,line*	change width of at least 1 field from defaults:

name=15		*file*=13	
function=15		*line*=20	

DATE — Print Current Date
% **date** [*option*] [+*format*]
Option:
–**u**	display date in GMT

output can be formatted with special characters:
%a	abbreviated weekday – **Sun** to **Sat**
%A	full weekday name
%b	abbreviated month name
%B	full month name
%c	country-specific date and time format
%d	day – **01** to **31**
%D	date as *mm/dd/yy*
%e	day of month – **1** to **31**
%h	same as **%b**
%H	hour – **00** to **23**
%I	hour – **01** to **12**
%j	Julian date – **001** to **366**
%m	month – **01** to **12**
%M	minute – **00** to **59**
%n	insert newline
%p	**AM** or **PM**

(continued)

DATE, continued

%r	time in AM/PM notation
%R	time as *hh*:*mm* (24-hour)
%S	second – **00** to **61**
%t	insert tab character
%T	time as *hh*:*mm*:*ss* (24-hour)
%U	week number – **00** to **53**
%w	day of week – Sun = **0**
%x	country-specific date format
%X	country-specific time format
%y	last 2 digits of year – **00** to **99**
%Y	4-digit year
%Z	time zone name

DC — Arbitrary Precision Desk Calculator
% **dc** [*file*]
   stdin read after *file*

DD — Convert and Copy File
% **dd** [*options*]
Options:

bs=*n*	both input and output block sizes
cbs=*n*	conversion buffer size (logical record length)
conv=	

	ascii	convert EBCDIC to ASCII
	block	convert to fixed length records
	ebcdic	convert ASCII to EBCDIC
	ibm	different ASCII to EBCDIC
	lcase	map upper case to lower
	noerror	continue on error
	swab	swap each pair of bytes
	sync	pad every record to value of **ibs**
	ucase	map lower case to upper
	unblock	
		convert to variable length records
	...,...	multiple conversions separated by commas

count=*n*	copy only *n* records
files=*n*	number of input files to copy (tape)
ibs=*n*	input block size (**512** default)
if=*file*	input filename (**stdin** default)
iseek=*n*	seek *n* input blocks (disk)
obs=*n*	output block size (**512** default)
of=*file*	output filename (**stdout** default)
oseek=*n*	seek *n* output records
seek=*n*	synonym for **oseek**
skip=*n*	skip *n* input blocks (tape)
n	number of bytes with optional suffix **k**, **b** or **w** to specify multiplication by 1024, 512, 2 or a product indicated by two numbers separated by an **x**

Θ **DELTA** — Install a Change into SCCS Files
% **delta** [*options*] *files*
   SCCS filenames read from **stdin** if *files* is –
Options:

– glist	*list* of deltas to ignore
– m[*list*]	*list* of Modification Request numbers
– n	save edited file
– p	print delta differences in **diff** format
– rsid	specify SCCS ID of delta

(continued)

DELTA, continued
  −s   suppress printing of new SCCS ID, etc.
  −y[*text*]   *text* inserted as comment

Δ **DEROFF** — Remove Formatter Constructs
% **deroff** [*options*] [*files*]
  stdin read if no *files* specified
Options:
  −m*x*   delete text from macro lines
                l   for **mm** macros, delete **mm** lists
                m   for **mm** macros
                s   for **ms** macros
  −w   build word list (1 word/line)

DF — Report Free Block Count
% **df** [*options*] [*filesys*]
Options:
  −b   print only k-bytes free
  −e   print only files free
  −f   print only free list count
  −F*type*   file system type (unmounted FSs)
  −g   print entire **statvfs** structure
  −k   print allocation in k-bytes
  −l   report on local file systems only
  −n   print only file system type
  −o*opts*   specify file system type specific options
  −t   print full listing with totals
  −V   echo command; don't execute

filesys   list of file systems, directories and
              mounted resources

DIFF — Differential File Comparer
% **diff** [*options*] *file1 file2*
  stdin read if − specified for *file1* or *file2*
  valid options are **bitw** and one of **cCDefhn**
% **diff** [*options*] *dir1 dir2*
  compare files in specified directories
  valid options are **bilrsStw** and one of **cefhn**
Options:
  −b   ignore trailing blanks, all whitespace equal
  −c   list differences with 3 lines of context
  −C *n*   same as **−c** with *n* lines
  −D *str*   create merged version of *file1* and *file2*
                with C preprocessor controls; **#define** *str*
                equivalent to compiling *file2*
  −e   produce **ed** script to make *file2* from *file1*
  −f   produce script to make *file2* from *file1*
                (not **ed** compatible)
  −h   do fast comparison (**−e** and **−f**
                not available)
  −i   ignore case of letters
  −l   produce long format output
  −n   produce **ed** script to make *file1* from *file2*;
                give count of changed lines
  −r   recursive **diff** on subdirectories
  −s   report identical files found
  −S *file*   start directory **diff** at *file*
  −t   expand TAB characters in output
  −w   ignore all blanks, strings of blanks equivalent

DIFF3 — Three-Way File Compare
% **diff3** [*options*] *file1 file2 file3*
Options:
−3	**ed** script for only lines with *file3* different
−e	**ed** script to add *file2* to *file3* changes to *file1*
−E	like **−e** but insert and flag overlapping changes
−x	**ed** script for only lines with all 3 files different
−X	like **−x** but insert and flag overlapping changes

Δ **DIFFMK** — Build "Change Mark" File for **n/troff**
% **diffmk** *old new change*

old	original file
new	updated file
change	change mark input for **n/troff**

DIRCMP — Compare Two Directories and Print Differences
% **dircmp** [*options*] *dir1 dir2*
Options:
−d	compare files with same names, make list to make files in *dir2* like those in *dir1*
−s	don't print messages about identical files
−w*n*	width of output line is *n* chars (**72** default)

DIRNAME — Delete End of Pathname (See **BASENAME**)
% **dirname** *string*

Θ **DIS** — Object Code Disassembler
% **dis** [*options*] *files*
Options:
−d *sect*	disassemble specified section, print offset of data from *sect* start
−D *sect*	disassemble specified section, print actual address of data
−F *function*	disassemble only *function*
−l *lib*	disassemble specified library
−L	put look-up of C source labels in symbol table
−o	print numbers in octal (hexadecimal default)
−s	perform symbolic disassembly
−t *sect*	disassemble *sect* as text
−V	print version information

DISABLE — Disable Specified Printers (See **LP**)
% **disable** [*option*] *printers*
Options:
−c	cancel jobs currently on *printers*
−r *reason*	apply *reason* to *printers* *reason* reported by **lpstat**
−W	wait for current request to complete

DOWNLOAD — Download PostScript Fonts
% **download** [*options*] [*files*]
Options:
−f	force complete scan of input file
−H *dir*	use *dir* as font directory (**/usr/lib/lp/postscript** default)

(continued)

DOWNLOAD, continued
- **m** *name*   specify font map table
- **p** *ptr*   first check resident font list
  /etc/lp/printers/*ptr***/residentfonts**

DPOST — **troff** postprocessor for PostScript
% **dpost** [*options*] [*files*]
Options:
- **c** *n*   print *n* copies of each page (**1** default)
- **e** *lev*   set text encoding level (**0**, **1** or **2**)
- **F** *dir*   specify font directory (**/usr/lib/font** default)
- **H** *dir*   specify host resident font directory
- **L** *pro*   use *pro* as prologue
  (**/usr/lib/postscript/dpost.ps** default)
- **m** *scale* scale page by *scale* uniformly about
  origin (1.0 default)
- **n** *n*   print *n* logical pages per physical page
- **o** *list*   print only listed page numbers
- **O**   disable picture inclusion
- **pl**   print in landscape mode
- **pp**   print in portrait mode (default)
- **T** *name* use font files for device *name* (**post** default)
- **w** *n*   set line width to *n* (**0.3** points default)
  upper left and lower right of sub-matrix
- **x** *xoff*   origin offset; positive means right
  (**0** inches default)
- **y** *yoff*   origin offset; positive means up
  (**0** inches default)

list   comma-separated, *n* – *m* means range,
       – *n* means beginning to page *n*, *n* – means
       from page *n* to end

Note: The origin is near the upper left corner of the page.

DSCONFIG — Display Data Storage Device Configuration
% **dsconfig** [*admin_name*]

admin_name   simple administration name for devices
           found in **/dev/rSA**

DU — Summarize Disk Usage
% **du** [*options*] [*directories*]
Options:
- **a**   generate entry for each file
  (directories only default)
- **r**   complain about directories that can't be read
- **s**   display only a grand total summary

Θ **DUMP** — Dump Object File or Archive Parts
% **dump** [*options*] *files*
Options: format is *option* [*modifiers*]
- **a**   dump archive header of each archive *file*
- **c**   dump string table
- **C**   dump decoded C++ symbol names
- **D**   dump debugging information
- **f**   dump *file* headers
- **g**   dump global symbols
- **h**   dump section headers
- **l**   dump line number information
- **L**   dump dynamic linking and shared lib info
- **o**   dump program execution header
- **r**   dump relocation information
- **s**   dump section contents in hex

DUMP, continued
−t	dump symbol table
−T*x1*[,*x2*]	dump symbol table entries specified by index *x1* or range from *x1* to *x2*
−u	internally convert **COFF** to **ELF**
−z *funct*	dump line numbers for *funct*

Option Modifiers:
−d *m*[,*n*]	dump section *m* or range *m* to *n*
−n *name*	dump info related to *name* (with **hrst**)
−p	don't print headers
−v	symbolic dump

ECHO — Echo Arguments
% **echo** [*args*]
Note: special escape conventions (place string in quotes)
\0*n*	character whose octal value is *n*
\b	backspace
\c	print line without newline
\f	form feed
\n	newline
\r	carriage return
\t	tab
\v	vertical tab
\\	backslash

ED — Text Editor (See Page 2)
% **ed** [*options*] [*file*]
Options:
−C	work with encrypted file (simulate C cmd)
−p *string*	specify prompt string
−s	suppress counts, diagnostics, etc.
−x	work with encrypted file (simulate X cmd)

EDIT — Line Text Editor
% **edit** [*options*] [*files*]
Options:
−C	work with encrypted file (simulate C cmd)
−r	recover file after crash
−x	work with encrypted file (simulate X cmd)

Θ **EFL** — Extended Fortran Language
% **efl** [*options*] [*files*]
Options:
−#	suppress comments in output program
−C	include comments in output program (default
−w	suppress warning messages
name = *value*	
	set *name* to *value* (i.e., **system** = **unix**)

EGREP — Search File for Pattern (See **GREP**)
% **egrep** [*options*] [*expr*] [*files*]
   stdin read if no *files* specified
Options:
−b	precede line with block number
−c	print count of matching lines only
−e *expr*	useful if the expression starts with a −
−f *file*	take expression from *file*
−h	don't print filenames
−i	ignore case
−l	print only names of files with matching lines
−n	print line numbers
−v	print non-matching lines

ENABLE — Activate Specified Printers (See **LP**)
% **enable** *printers*

ENV — Alter Environment and Execute Command
% **env** [*options*] [*command* [*args*]]
Options:
      –   set environment only to specified values
    name = *value*
                      set environment variable *name* to *value*

args   passed to *command*

Δ **EQN** — Format Mathematical Text for **troff**
% **eqn** [*options*] [*files*]
    stdin read if no *files* specified
Options:
    – dxy set start delimiter to x and end
                delimiter to y
    – fn set to font n
    – pn set sub- and superscripts in point size n
    – sn set in point size n
    – Tdev format for *device*

EX — Text Editor
% **ex** [*options*] [*files*]
Options:
    + *pos*   position file at *pos*
    –   suppress diagnostics, counts, etc.
    – c *cmd* execute *cmd* in editor
    – C   work with encrypted file (simulate C cmd)
    – l   set options for editing LISP files
    – L   list filenames of files saved in crash
    – r *file*   retrieve last saved version of
                named file after system or editor crash
    – R   set **readonly** option
    – s   suppress counts, diagnostics, etc.
    – t *tag*   edit file containing *tag* and position editor
                at its definition
    – v   equivalent to using **vi**
    – x   work with encrypted file (simulate X cmd)

pos   any editor command not containing a space

EXPR — Evaluate Expression Arguments
% **expr** *args*
Binary operators:
    \| return first operand if first is not null or 0
    \&   return first operand if neither is null or 0
    =, \>, \>=, \<, \<=, !=
                integer comparison operators
    +, -, *, /, %
                integer arithmetic operators
    :   match operator - returns number of bytes
                matched or use \(. . . \) to return portion
                of first operand.

EXSTR — Extract Strings from C Source
% **exstr** [*options*] *files*
Options:
–d	at run time, print message if **gettxt()** fails
–e	include position information in extraction
–r	replace strings with calls to **gettxt()**

Θ **F77** — Fortran 77 Compiler
% **f77** [*options*] *files*
Options:
–1	DO loops performed at least once
–66	don't enhance Fortran 66 compatibility
–c	suppress link edit; produce **.o** files
–C	set up for run-time subscript range checking
–E	use remaining chars of argument as **efl** flags
–f	use floating point software
–F	run **efl** or **ratfor** and produce **.o** files only
–g	enable **sdb** debugger (VAX only)
–m	apply **m4** preprocessor to **efl** and **ratfor** files
–o *output*	name of output file (**a.out** default)
–onetrip	same as **–1**
–O	invoke object code optimizer
–p	set up object files for profiling
–R	use remaining chars of arg as **ratfor** flags
–S	produce assembly language **.s** files only
–u	set default variable type to undefined
–U	treat upper and lower case as separate
–v	display diagnostics for each process
–w	suppress warnings
–w66	suppress Fortran 66 compatibility warnings

FACE — Framed Access Command Environment
% **face** [*options*] [*files*]
Options:
–a *afile*	specify alias file
–c *cfile*	modify FMLI commands with *cfile*
–i *ifile*	specify initialization file

files is a full pathname for file describing object being
opened initially; if no *files* specified opens objects specified
by **LOGINWIN** environment variable from **.environ** file.

Naming convention:
Menu.*xxx*	menu
Form.*xxx*	form
Text.*xxx*	text file

FACTOR — Print Prime Factors of a Number
% **factor** [*n*]
n	**stdin** read if *n* not specified

FALSE — Return Unsuccessful Exit Status (See **TRUE**)
% **false**

FGREP — Search File for Pattern (See **GREP**)
% **fgrep** [*options*] [*strings*] [*files*]
    stdin read if no *files* specified
Options:
–b	precede line with block number
–c	print count of matching lines only
–e *expr*	useful if expression starts with a **–**
–f *file*	take *string* from *file*
–h	suppress print of filenames

FGREP, continued
          -i   ignore case of letters
          -l   print only names of files with matching lines
          -n   print line numbers
          -s   silent, only print error messages
          -v   print non-matching lines
          -x   print exact matches (whole line) only

strings   list of strings separated by (escaped) newlines
          and enclosed in single quotes defining the list of
          patterns to search for

FILE — Attempt to Classify Files
% **file** [*option*] *files*
Option:
          -c   check magic file for format errors
          -f *nfile*   use *nfile* as a file of filenames
          -h   don't follow symbolic links
          -m *magic* use alternate magic file (**/etc/magic** default)

FIND — Find Files
% **find** *pathname-list expression*
Expressions: formed from one or more primaries
Primaries:
          -atime *n* true if file found was accessed *n* days ago
          -ctime *n* true if file found was changed *n* days ago
          -depth   always true; causes entries in directory to
                          be acted on before the directory itself
          -exec *cmd*
                          execute *cmd*, true if successful exit status;
                          replace {} by current pathname;
                          command must end with ";"
          -follow   always true; follow symbolic links
          -fstype *type*
                          true if file in filesystem of specified type
          -group *name*
                          true if file found is owned by the group *name*
          -inum *n*   true if file has inode number *n*
          -links *n* true if file found has *n* links
          -local   true if file is on local system
          -mount   don't cross mounted file systems,
                          always true
          -mtime *n* true if file found was modified *n* days ago
          -name *pat*
                          true if *pat* matches name of file found
          -newer *file*
                          true if file found modified after *file*
          -nogroup true if file group not in group file
          -nouser   true if file owner not in password file
          -ok *cmd*   like **-exec** except user prompted first
          -perm [-]*octal*
                          true if permission of file found is *octal*
                          – forces true if any bits in *octal* match a
                          file permission
          -prune   do not continue down tree
          -print   print name of files found, always true
          -size *n*[**c**] true if file found is *n* blocks [characters] long
          -type *c*   true if file found is:
                          b   block special file
                          c   character special file
                          d   directory

(continued)

FIND, continued

f	plain file
l	symbolic link
p	fifo or named pipe

–user *name*
    true if file found is owned by user or ID *name*

\(*expr* \) true if *expr* is true, used for grouping

n   *n* means exactly *n*, **+**n means more than *n*, **–**n means less than *n*

Ways to join primaries:
! *expr*   negate truth value of *expr*
exp1 exp2 true if both *exp1* and *exp2* are true
exp1 **–o** *exp2*
    true if either *exp1* or *exp2* is true

pathname-list directories where search is to begin

FINGER — Find Information about Users
% **finger** [*options*] [*users*]
% **finger** [–l] *users* [**@**hosts]
Options:

–b	in-between size output format
–f	suppress header
–h	suppress printing **.project** file
–i	just show idle time for *users*
–l	long output format
–m	match *user* to login name only
–p	don't show information from **.plan** file
–q	quick list of users
–s	short output format
–w	like **–s** but don't show full name

FMLI — Form and Menu Language Interpreter
% **fmli** [*options*] *files*
Options:

–a *alias*	specify alias file
–c *cfile*	modify FMLI commands with *cfile*
–i *init*	initialization file specifying characteristics of application including transient introductory frame, banner, color attributes and Screen Labeled Keys (SLKs)

FMT — Simple Text Formatter
% **fmt** [*options*] *files*
Options:

–c	crown margin mode; preserve indentation of first two lines, align to second line
–s	split only; don't join short lines
–w *n*	fill output up to *n* columns

FMTMSG — Display Message on **stderr** or Console
% **fmtmsg** [*options*] *text*
Options:

–a *action*	"to fix" description
–c *class*	source of message
	firm firmware condition
	hard hardware condition
	soft software condition
–l *from*	source of the message

(continued)

    −s *severity* seriousness of error

                error   fault detected
                halt   fatal error
                info   information only; not error
                warn   abnormal condition

    −t *tag*   message identifier

    −u *subclass*

            comma-separated list from below:
            appl   condition originated in application
            console write message to console
            nrecov application will not recover
            opsys   condition originated in kernel
            print   print message to **stderr**
            recov   application will recover
            util   condition originated in utility

text   text string describing condition (write so it appears as a single argument to program)

FOLD — Fold Long Lines
% **fold** [*option*] *files*
stdin read if no *files* specified
Options:
    −w *n*   fold to *n* columns (80 default)

FSPLIT — Split Fortran File
% **fsplit** [*options*] *files*
Options:
    −e   use **efl** input files
    −f   use **f77** input files (default)
    −r   use **ratfor** input files
    −s   remove trailing blanks, make **f77** lines ≤ 72 characters

FTP — File Transfer Program
% **ftp** [*options*] [*hostname*]
Options:
    −d   enable debugging
    −g   disable filename expansion
    −i   disable interactive prompting
    −n   disable auto-login
    −t   enable packet tracing (ignored)
    −v   show all remote responses (default if interactive)

FTP Commands
    ! [*cmd*]   run *cmd* on local machine
                if no *cmd*, spawn interactive shell
    $ *mac* [*args*]
                execute macro *mac* w/optional *args*
    account [*passwd*]
                supply supplemental password
    ? [*cmd*]   same as **help**
    append *local_file* [*remote_file*]
                append *local_file* to *remote_file*
    ascii   set representation type to network ASCII
    bell   sound bell after each file transfer
    binary   set representation type to image
    bye   terminate session with remote and exit **ftp**
    case   toggle case mapping (off default)
    cd *rdir*   change to *rdir* on remote system

(continued)

cdup	move "up" one directory on remote
close	terminate session with remote; return to command interpreter
cr	toggle <cr> stripping during ASCII retrieval
delete *rfile*	
	delete *rfile* on remote system
debug	toggle debugging mode
dir [*rdir*] [*lfile*]	
	list remote directory contents; optionally put output in *lfile*
disconnect	
	same as **close**
form [*format*]	
	set carriage control format subtype
get *rfile* [*lfile*]	
	retrieve *rfile*; store on local system
glob	toggle file name expansion
hash	toggle # display for each block transferred
help [*cmd*]	get help with *cmd*; if no *args*, print command summary
lcd [*dir*]	change directory on local system (**$HOME** default)
ls [*rdir*] [*lfile*]	
	short directory listing on remote system; output to *lfile* (terminal default)
macdef *mname*	
	all input until blank line becomes definition of macro *mname*
	use **$n** to refer to parameters
	use **$i** to loop through parameters
mdelete [*rfiles*]	
	delete *rfiles* on remote system
mdir *rfiles file*	
	multi-file **dir**; output to *file*
mget *rfiles*	
	get multiple files from remote system
mkdir *rdir*	make directory on remote system
mls *rfiles lfile*	
	multi-file **ls**; output to *lfile*
mode [**stream**]	
	set transfer mode to **stream**
mput *lfiles*	
	expand wild cards and execute **put** for each file
nmap [*in out*]	
	set filename mapping; if no arguments, unset
ntrans [*in* [*out*]]	
	set the filename character translation: if no arguments, unset
open *host* [*port*]	
	connect to *host*; optional port number may be supplied
prompt	toggle interactive prompting
proxy *ftp_cmd*	
	execute ftp command on secondary connection
put *lfile* [*rfile*]	
	store local file on remote machine (*rfile* defaults to "mapped" *lfile*)
pwd	print current directory name on remote

(continued)

FTP, continued

quit	same as **bye**
quote *arg1 arg2*	
	send args to remote server
recv *rfile* [*lfile*]	
	same as **get**
remotehelp [*cmd*]	
	get help from remote server
rename *file1 file2*	
	rename *file1* as *file2* on remote
reset	clear reply queue
rmdir *rdir*	remove directory on remote system
runique	toggle local unique filename mapping
send *lfile* [*rfile*]	
	same as **put**
sendport	toggle use of PORT commands
status	show current status of ftp
struct [**file**]	
	set file structure
sunique	toggle remote unique filename mapping
tenex	set to talk to TENEX systems
trace	toggle packet tracing (unimplemented)
type [*type*]	set representation type; types are **ascii**, **binary**, **image** (**ascii** default)
user *username* [*passwd*] [*accnt*]	
	sign on to remote server
verbose	toggle verbose mode

GCORE — Get Core Image of Processes
% **gcore** *option PIDs*
Option:

−o *file*	core images to *file.PID* (**core.***PID* default)

GENCAT — Generate Formatted Message Catalog
% **gencat** [*options*] *cfile mfiles*
Options:

−f *fmt*	specify catalog format	
	m	equivalent to **−m** option
	SVR4	produce SVR4 format catalog (default)
	XENIX	produce catalogs for SCO UNIX/XENIX applications
−m	generate *cfile* compatible with earlier versions	

cfile	catalog file to be created
mfiles	files of messages to catalog

Θ **GET** — Retrieve an SCCS File Version
% **get** [*options*] *files*
    SCCS filenames read from **stdin** if *files* is −
Options:

−a*n*	specify delta sequence number retrieved
−b	create new branch (**−e** required)
−c*when*	do not include deltas made after *when* (format: *YY*[*MM*[*DD*[*HH*[*MM*[*SS*]]]]])
−e	retrieve the version for editing
−g	suppress version retrieval
−i*list*	*list* of deltas to include
−k	SCCS ID keywords not replaced
−l	delta summary written to **l.***file***.c**
−lp	delta summary written to **stdout**

(continued)

GET, continued
       −m   precede each line with its related SCCS ID
       −n   precede each line with **%M%** ID keyword
       −p   retrieved version written to **stdout**
       −r*sid*   specify SCCS ID of version
       −s   suppress **stdout** output
       −t   access most recent delta
       −w *string* substitute *string* for **%W%**
       −x*list*   *list* of deltas to exclude

GETOPT — Parse Command Options
(being replaced by **getopts**)
% **set −− 'getopt** *string* **$ * '**

string   list of recognized option letters

GETOPTCVT — Convert From **getopt** to **getopts**
% **/usr/lib/getoptcvt** [*option*] *file*
Option:
       −b   make backward-compatible script

GETOPTS — Parse Command Options
% **getopts** *string var* [*args*]

args   parse *args*
var   shell variable to place next option in
string   list of recognized option letters; followed
             by : if option has argument

GETTXT — Get String from Message Database
% **gettxt** *mfile***:***mnum* [*default_MSG*]

GLOSSARY — Definitions of UNIX Terms
% **help glossary**
     display glossary menu
% **glossary** *term*
     give definition of *term*

Δ **GREEK** — Set Up Extended Character Set Filter
% **greek** (**−T***term*]
     $TERM default
Terminals:
       −300   DASI 300
       −300-12   DASI 300 in 12 pitch
       −300s   DASI 300s
       −300s-12   DASI 300s in 12 pitch
       −450   DASI 450
       −450-12   DASI 450 in 12 pitch
       −1620   Diablo 1620
       −1620-12   Diablo 1620 in 12 pitch
       −2621   same as **hp**
       −2640   same as **hp**
       −2645   same as **hp**
       −4014   same as **tek**
       −hp   HP 2621, 2640, and 2645
       −tek   Tektronix 4014

GREP — Search File for Pattern (See **EGREP**, **FGREP**)
% **grep** [*options*] *pattern* [*files*]
　　stdin read if no *files* specified
(See Page 88 For Regular Expressions)
Options:
–b	precede line with block number (0 is first block)
–c	print count of matching lines only
–h	suppress print of filenames
–i	ignore case of letters in comparisons
–l	print only names of files with matching lines
–n	print line numbers
–s	suppress file error messages
–v	print non-matching lines

GROUPS — Display Group Membership of User
% **groups** [*user*]

HEAD — Print First Lines of File
% **head** [*option*] [*files*]
　stdin read if no *files* specified
Option:
–n	print first *n* lines (**10** default)

Θ **HELP** — Explain a Message or SCCS Command
% **help** [*args*]
　args　　SCCS commands or message numbers
　help stuck display info on using **help**

HP — Handle Special Functions of HP2640 &2621
% **hp** [*options*]
Options:
–e	use display enhancements mode
–m	convert >2 consecutive newlines to 2

HPIO — HP 2645A Terminal Tape File Archiver
% **hpio** – **i**[*options*] [– **n** *n*]
　　copy in: extract *files* from tape
% **hpio** – **o**[*options*] *files*
　　copy out: copy *files* to tape
Copy in options:
a	query before creating a file
–n *n*	extract *n* input files (**1** default)
r	use right tape drive
t	print table of contents only

Copy out options:
c	include checksum at end of each *file*
r	use right tape drive

△ **HYPHEN** — Find Hyphenated Words and Print
% **hyphen** [*files*]
　　stdin read if no *files* specified

ICONV — Code Set Converter
% **iconv** – **f** *from_code* – **t** *to_code* [*file*]
　stdin read if no *files* specified

ID — Print User and Group IDs and Names
% **id** [*option*]
Option:
–a	report all groups to which user belongs

Θ **INSTALL** — Install Commands
% **/usr/sbin/install** [*options*] *file* [*dirs*]
Options:
- **−c** *dir*   install in *dir* if not found
- **−f** *dir*   force install in *dir*
- **−g** *group*   set group ID of installed file (superuser only)
- **−i**   ignore default directory search list
- **−m** *mode*   set mode of new file
- **−n** *dir*   if *file* not found, install in *dir*
- **−o**   copy "found" copy to **OLD***file*
- **−s**   suppress printing of non-error messages
- **−u** *user*   set owner of installed file (superuser only)

file   file to install (by overwriting)
dirs   directories to search for file (**/bin**, **/usr/bin**, **/etc**, **/lib**, **/usr/lib** default)

IPCRM — Remove Inter-Process Communications Items
% **ipcrm** [*options*]
Options:
- **−m** *mem*   remove shared memory ID and structure
- **−M** *mkey*   remove shared memory structure created with *mkey*
- **−q** *msg*   remove message queue ID and structure
- **−Q** *qkey*   remove message queue structure created with *qkey*
- **−s** *sem*   remove semaphore ID and structure
- **−S** *skey*   remove semaphore structure created with *skey*

IPCS — Print Inter-Process Communication Facility Status
% **ipcs** [*options*]
Options:
- **−a**   include all print options (**bcopt**)
- **−b**   report info about maximum allowable sizes
- **−c**   report creator's login and group name
- **−C** *core*   use *core* for reporting (**/dev/kmem** default)
- **−m**   report on active shared memory segments
- **−N** *list*   report on processes in *list* (**/stand/unix** default)
- **−o**   current message & shared memory usage
- **−p**   report PIDs of recently active processes
- **−q**   report on active message queues
- **−s**   report on active semaphores
- **−t**   report time info on recently active processes

ISMPX — Return Windowing Terminal State
% **ismpx** [*option*]
Option:
- **−s**   return only exit status

JOIN — Form the Join of Two Relations
% **join** [*options*] *file1 file2*
    stdin read if − specified for *file1*
Options:
- **−a***n*   produce line for each unpairable line in *filen*
- **−e** *str*   replace empty fields with string *str*
- **−j***n m*   join on *m*th field of *filen*

(continued)

JOIN, continued
  - **o** *list*   specify output fields; each element of form:
                 n.m where *n* is file and *m* is field;
                 list is space-separated
  - **t***c*   use *c* as field separator (**tab** default)

JSH — Job Control Shell (see **SH**)
% **jsh** [*options*] [*args*]

JTERM — Reset Layer of Windowing Terminal
% **jterm**

JWIN — Print Window Size of Layer
% **jwin**

KILL — Terminate or Send a Signal to Processes
% **kill** [*option*] *PIDs*
    send signal to process
% **kill** *option* –*PGIDs*
    send signal to all members of process groups
% **kill –l**
    list available signals
Option:
  - *signo*   decimal number of signal sent (**15** default)
  common signals are:

1	hangup
2	interrupt
3	quit
4	illegal instruction
5	trace trap
6	IOT instruction
7	EMT instruction
8	floating point exception
9	kill (cannot be caught or ignored)
10	bus error
11	segmentation violation
12	bad system call argument
13	write on unread pipe
14	alarm clock
15	software termination signal
16	user defined signal 1
17	user defined signal 2

PIDs   process IDs to receive the signal (**0** implies all
            processes resulting from current login)
PGIDs   process IDs of group leader

KSH — Korn Shell
% **ksh** [*options*] [*args*]
Options:
  - **a**   automatically export vars when defined
  - **c** *cmd*   execute *cmd*
  - **e**   exit on error (after executing ERR trap)
  - **f**   disable file name generation
  - **h**   make command into tracked alias
  - **i**   force interactive mode
  - **k**   place variables in environment for command
  - **m**   run background jobs as separate
                 process group
  - **n**   parse commands without executing them

(continued)

KSH, continued
  −o *opt*   set options; can occur multiple times
                allexport same as **−a**
                errexit same as **−e**
                bgnice lower priority of background jobs
                ignoreeof don't exit on EOF
                keyword same as **−k**
                markdirs append / to generated directory
                    names
                monitor same as **−m**
                noclobber prevent > from clobbering
                    existing file
                noexec same as **−n**
                noglob same as **−f**
                nolog don't save function defs in history file
                nounset same as **−u**
                privileged same as **−p**
                trackall same as **−h**
                verbose same as **−v**
                vi enter vi-style in-line editor
                viraw process each character in vi mode
                xtrace same as **−x**
  −p   disable processing **.profile**
  −r   run in restricted (**rsh**) mode
  −s   sort positional parameters lexicographically
  −t   exit after executing one command
  −u   treat unset parameters as error
  −v   echo shell input as read
  −x   print commands as they are executed

Note: + instead of − before option turns that option off.

LAST — Display Last Logins
% **last** [*options*] [*names*]
Options:
  −*n*   limit output to *n* entries
  −f *file*   use *file* instead of **/var/adm/wtmp**
  −n *n*   same as **−***n*

names   can be login names or terminals

LAYERS — Manage Windows
% **layers** [*options*] [*program*]
Options:
  −d   print size of firmware patch on **stderr**,
               if downloaded
  −D   print debugging messages on **stderr**
  −f *file*   use configuration in *file* for layer
  −h *mods*   comma delimited list of STREAMS modules
               to connect channel
  −m *size*   maximum packet size
  −p   print statistics on firmware patch on **stderr**,
               if downloaded
  −s   report statistics on **stderr** upon exiting
  −t   print trace dump on **stderr** upon exiting

program   firmware patch to download to terminal before
            creating layer

Θ **LD** — Linkage Editor
% **ld** [*options*] *files*
Options:
    –a   create an absolute file (static only)
    –b   make more efficient, less sharable code
                (dynamic only)
    –Bdynamic
                link with **.so** library
    –Bstatic   link with **.a** library
    –Bsymbolic
                symbolic bind (dynamic only)
    –dn   static linking
    –dy   dynamic linking (default)
    –e *symb* set default entry point to value of *symb*
    –f *fill*   set default fill pattern to *fill*
    –G   produce shared object instead of
                dynamic link
    –h *name* use *name* as dynamic link name
    –I *name* specify interpreter for program header
    –l *x*   search **lib**x**.so** or **lib**x**.a**
    –L *dir*   add *dir* to library search list
    –m   print memory map
    –M *map* use *map* as link directives
    –N   put data after text in output file
    –o *output* name of output file (**a.out** default)
    –Qn   suppress tool ID information
    –Qy   put tool ID information in output (default)
    –r   generate relocatable (**ld**able) output
    –s   strip output of symbol table and
                relocation bits
    –t   don't warn about multiply-defined symbols
    –u *symb* enter *symb* as undefined symbol
    –V   print version information
    –VS *n*   put version number *n* in output file header
    –x   don't preserve local symbols in table
    –Y[*lib*],*dir* use *dir* instead of default *lib*rary
                lib   **L** = **/lib**, **U** = **/usr/lib**
    –YP,*dirlist* use *dirlist* (colon separated) instead of
                default *lib*
    –z defs   force error on undefined symbol
    –z nodefsallow undefined symbols
    –z text   force error if relocations against
                non-writable allocatable section
    –Z   don't bind anything to address zero

Θ **LDD** — List Dynamic Dependencies
% **ldd** [*option*] *file*
Options:
    –d   check all references to data objects
    –r   check all references to data objects and
                functions

Θ **LEX** — Generate Lexical Analysis Programs
% **lex** [*options*] [*files*]
    stdin read if no *files* specified
Options:
    –c   **C** actions (default)
    –n   don't print out summary
    –Qn   suppress tool ID information (default)
    –Qy   put tool ID information in output
    –r   **ratfor** actions
    –t   output to **stdout** instead of **lex.yy.c**

LEX, continued

-v	provide summary statistics
-V	print version information

LINE — Copy One Line from **stdin** to **stdout**
% **line**

Θ **LINT** — C Program Checker
% **lint** [*options*] *files*
Options:

-a	suppress messages about assignment of longs to non-longs
-b	suppress messages about unreachable **breaks**
-c	put output of first pass in **.ln** file
-D *name* [*=def*]	define *name* as *def* (**1** default)
-F	print pathnames of files
-g	enable **sdb** debugger
-h	don't apply heuristic tests
-I*dir*	search *dir* before standard ones
-k	print "lint comments"
-l*x*	include lint library **llib-l***x***.ln**
-L*dir*	search lint libraries in *dir* first
-m	suppress complaints about externals that could be static
-n	don't check compatibility against libraries
-o*lib*	create library **llib-l***lib***.ln**
-O	optimize object code produced
-p	check portability with other C dialects
-R*file*	write **.ln** file to *file* (for **cxref**)
-s	print one-line diagnostics only
-u	suppress messages about undefined or unused functions and external variables
-U*symb*	remove definition of *symb*
-v	suppress messages about unused arguments
-V	print version information
-W*file*	write **.ln** file to *file* (for **cflow**)
-x	don't report unused variables declared external
-y	pretend /*LINTLIBRARY*/ directive found

Most **cc** command-line options are recognized or ignored.

Θ **LIST** — Produce C Source Listing from Common Object File
% **list** [*options*] *source* [*object*]
    a.out used if no *object* given
Options:

-F*function*	list only *function*
-h	don't print headers
-v	print version information of **list** on **stderr**

LISTUSERS — List User Login Information
% **listusers** [*options*]
Options:

-g *groups*	list users belonging to *groups*
-l *logins*	list users with specified *logins*

    groups and *logins* can be comma-delimited lists

LN — Make Links to Files (See **CP**)
% **ln** [*option*] *file1 file2*
    make a link to *file1* named *file2*
% **ln** [*option*] *files directory*
    make links of specified *files* in *directory*
Option:
    – f   force link despite target file permissions
    – n   don't overwrite existing file
    – s   create symbolic link

LOCATE — Identify a UNIX Command
% **locate** [*keywords*]
    without *keywords* displays the **locate** screen
    keywords   functions, i.e., "print file"

LOGIN — Sign On to System
% **login** [*user*] [*sets*]
    login *user*, logout if no *user* specified

sets are of the form *env_var=value* to set environment
variables (not **$PATH** or **$SHELL**)

LOGNAME — Print Login Name
% **logname**
    print value of **$LOGNAME** environment variable

Θ **LORDER** — Find Ordering Relation for Archive Files
% **lorder** *files*

LP — Send Request to Printer
% **lp** [*options*] *files*
% **lp –i** *request* [*options*]
    change options of queued request
Options:
    – c   copy rather than link files
    – d *ptr*   send request to specified printer
    – f *form* [**– d any**]
                    print on form *form*
    – H *special-handling*
                    hold suspend request
                    immediate print request next
                    resume resume held request
    – i *request* apply option changes to *request*
    – m   send mail after printing
    – n *n*   print *n* copies (**1** default)
    – o *option*   specify printer- or class-dependent options
    – P *page-list*
                    print specified pages
    – q *pri*   assign specified priority (**0** to **39**; **0** is highest)
    – s   suppress messages from **lp**
    – S *char-set* [**– d any**]
                    print with specified character set
    – t *title*   print *title* on banner page of output
    – T *content_type* [**–r**]
                    print on printer that supports content_type;
                    –r indicates don't use filter
    – w   write to user's terminal after printing
    – y *modes*   print according to mode list

Θ **LPROF** — Print Execution Profile
% **lprof** [*options*]
% **lprof – m** *files*.**cnt** [**– T**] **– d** *ofile*.**cnt**
  merge profile data files into *ofile*.**cnt**
Options:
– c *cfile*	use *cfile*.**cnt** as input (*prog*.**cnt** default)
– I *idir*	add *idir* to list of included directories
– o *prog*	use *prog* as program overriding name in profile file
– p	print listing
– r *sfiles*	print listing for *sfiles* only
– s	print summary information
– T	timestamp override for merge mode
– V	print version information
– x	display report showing lines not executed

LPSTAT — Print Status of Printer System
% **lpstat** [*options*]
Options:
– a [*list1*]	print acceptance status of destinations
– c [*classnames*]	print *classnames* and members
– d	print default destination for **lp**
– f [*forms*] [**–l**]	verify that specified forms are recognized (**all** default) −l lists form descriptions
– o [*list2*]	print status of printer requests
– p [*ptrs*] [**– D**] [**–l**]	print status of specified printers −**D** print printer description list −l print full description for local printers
– r	print information on the **lp** request scheduler
– R	show position of job in queue
– s	print summary system statistics
– S [*csets*] [**–l**]	verify that specified character sets are recognized (**all** default) −l append list of devices
– t	print all status information
– u [*users*]	print information on *user*'s requests
– v [*ptrs*]	print list of pathnames for printers
list1	list of printer and class names
list2	list of printer names, class names, request IDs
users	may include system name (**all** means all)

LS — List Contents of Directories
% **ls** [*options*] [*directories*]
  current working directory used if no *directories* specified
Options:
– 1	print one entry per line
– a	list all entries (including ones starting with .)
– b	print non-printing characters as octal
– c	use time file created in **– t** & **– l** options
– C	multi-column output with entries sorted down
– d	list only name (not contents) of directory
– f	interpret each argument as directory
– F	print / after directories, * after executables, @ after symbolic links
– g	like **– l** but don't print owner

−i	print i-node number
−l	long list (mode, links, owner, group, size, modification time)
−L	list file referenced by link (instead of link itself)
−m	print files across, separated by commas
−n	like **−l** but use numeric user and group IDs
−o	like **−l** but don't print group
−p	mark directories with /
−q	print non-printing characters as a **?**
−r	reverse sort order
−R	recursively list subdirectories
−s	print size in blocks
−t	sort by modification time
−u	use time of last access in **−t** & **−l** options
−x	multi-column list, sorted across each row

Θ **M4** — Macro Preprocessor
% **m4** [*options*] [*files*]
    stdin read if − or no *files* specified
Options:

−B*n*	size of push-back & arg buffers (**4096** default)
−D*name* [=*val*]	define *name* to *val* (**null** default)
−e	operate interactively
−H*n*	hash array size *n* (**199** default)
−s	enable line sync output for C preprocessor
−S*n*	call stack size (**100** default)
−T*n*	token buffer size (**512** default)
−U*name*	undefine *name*

MAIL — Send or Read Mail
% **mail** [*options*] *users*
    send message from **stdin** to *users*
Send Mail Options:

−m *mtype*	add **Message-Type:** *mtype*
−o	don't optimize address
−s	don't add newline at top of letter
−t	include list of people to send mail to in **To:** lines
−w	don't wait for completion of remote transfer program to send to remote user

% **mail** [*options*]
Read Mail Options:

−e	check for mail, return 0 if mail is present **1** if no mail
−f*file*	read messages from *file*, (**mbox** default)
−F*users*	forward mail to *users* (use in *mailbox*)
−h	print headers only
−p	print all messages, no prompt for disposition
−P	print all messages, all header lines
−q	terminate after interrupt
−r	print messages in first-in, first-out order

% **mail −F** *users*
    forward incoming mail to *users*

MAILALIAS — Display Mail Alias Names
% **mailalias** [*options*] *names*
Options:
-s	don't prefix lines with *name*
-v	send debugging info to **stdout**

MAILX — Send or Read Mail (See **MAIL**)
% **mailx** [*options*] *users*
    send message from **stdin** to *users*
Send Mail Options:
-d	show debugging output
-F	record output in file named *user1*
-h *n*	*n* network hops made so far
-i	ignore interrupts
-n	disable reading of **/etc/mail/mailx.rc**
-r *address*	pass *address* to network software
-s *subject*	set subject heading to *subject*
-U	convert UUCP address to internet format
-V	print version information

% **mailx** [*options*]
Read Mail Options:
-e	check for mail, return **0** if mail is present
-f [*file*]	read messages from *file* (**mbox** default)
-H	only print header summary
-I	include group and ID header lines in output
-n	disable reading of **/etc/mail/mailx.rc**
-N	don't print header summary
-T *file*	record headers in *file*
-u *user*	read *user*'s mail
-V	print version information

Θ **MAKE** — Maintain Program Groups
% **make** [*options*] [*names*]
Options:
-b	old *makefile* compatibility mode
-d	print detailed debugging information
-e	environment variables override **makefile**
-f *makefile*	specify name of description file (**makefile**, **Makefile**, **s.makefile**, **s.Makefile** defaults) *makefile* named – uses **stdin**
-i	ignore errors of invoked commands
-k	abort current entry on error; continue with unrelated entries
-n	print but don't execute commands
-p	print macro definitions and target descriptions
-q	successful exit status if target file is current
-r	do not use built-in rules
-s	do not print commands before executing
-t	update target files by **touch**ing them
-u	force unconditional update

MAKEKEY — Make Encryption Key
% **/usr/lib/makekey**

Δ **MAN** — Print Manual Entries
% **man** [*options*] [*section*] *titles*
Options:
-12	produce 12 pitch output
-c	invoke **col** to process output

(continued)

MAN, continued

−d	search current directory instead of **/usr/manV**
−s	typeset in small (6"x9") format
−t	typeset in default (8.5"x11") format
−T *term*	format using **nroff** for terminal type *term* (**450** default)
−w	print only pathnames of entries
−y	use non-compacted macros

Θ **MCS** — Manipulate Comment Section of Object File
% **mcs** [*options*] *file*
Options:

−a *string*	append *string* to comment section
−c	compress comment section
−d	delete comment section
−n *section*	access *section* (**.comment** default)
−p	print comment section
−V	print version information

MESG — Permit or Deny Messages via **write** or **talk**
% **mesg** [*option*]
   current message state printed if no *option* specified
Options:

−n	deny messages
−y	allow messages

MKDIR — Create Specified Directories
% **mkdir** [*options*] *dirnames*
Options:

−m *mode*	specify directory's mode (see **chmod**)
−p	create parent directories that don't exist

MKMSGS — Create Message Files from Strings
% **mkmsgs** [*options*] *stringfile msgfile*
Options:

−i *locale*	put *msgfile* in directory **/usr/lib/locale/***locale***/LC_MESSAGES**
−o	overwrite *msgfile*

Θ **MKSHLIB** — Make a Shared Library
% **mkshlib** [*options*]
Options:

−h *host*	host shared library is *host*
−n	don't generate new target shared library
−q	suppress warning messages
−s *file*	specification file is *file*
−t *target*	target shared library is is *target*

Δ **MM** — Print MM Format Documents
% **mm** [*options*] [*files*]
   option list is printed if no arguments specified
Options:

−12	use 12 pitch print
−c	invoke **col** (default except for fancy printers)
−cm	use compacted macros
−e	invoke **neqn**
−E	invoke **−e** option of **nroff**
−mm	use noncompacted version of macros
−t	invoke **tbl**
−T*term*	specify terminal type (**$TERM** default)
−y	use non-compacted macros

43

(continued)

MM, continued
Any other options are passed to **nroff**.

Δ **MMT** — Typeset MM Format Documents
% **mmt** [*options*] [*files*]
    stdin read if – specified in *files*
Options:

– a	invoke the **– a** option of **troff**
– D*dest*	specify output destination
– e	invoke **eqn**
– p	invoke **pic**
– t	invoke **tbl**
– T*term*	specify terminal type (**$TERM** default)
– y	use non-compacted macros
– z	don't direct output through post-processor

Any other options are passed to **troff** or macro package.

MORE — View File by Screenful or by Line
% **more** [*options*] [*files*]
Options:

+ /*pat*	start 2 lines before line containing **pat**
– c	redraw instead of scroll
– d	display error message on invalid command
– f	count by <newlines> instead of screen lines
– l	treat formfeed (^L) as ordinary character
– *n*	window size (default set with **stty**)
+ *n*	start viewing file at line *n*
– r	display control characters as ^C
– s	reduce multiple blank lines to one
– u	suppress terminal underlining or enhancing
– w	prompt before exiting (any key terminates)

Entering **?** or **h** shows summary of **more** commands.

MV — Move Files (See **CP**)
% **mv** [*options*] *file1 file2*
    rename (or move) *file1* to *file2*
% **mv** [*options*] *files directory*
    rename (or move) specified *files* to *directory*
Options:

– f	force move despite target file permissions
– i	ask for confirmation before overwriting target

Δ **MVT** — Typeset Viewgraphs (See **MMT**)
% **mvt** [*options*] [*files*]
    option list printed if no arguments specified
    stdin read if – specified in *files*
Options:

– a	invoke the **– a** option of **troff**
– D*dest*	specify output destination
– e	invoke **eqn**
– p	invoke **pic**
– t	invoke **tbl**
– T*term*	specify terminal type (**$TERM** default)
– y	use non-compacted macros
– z	don't direct output through post-processor

Any other options are passed to **troff** or macro package.

NAWK — Pattern Scanning Language (See Page 80)
% **nawk** [*options*] [*prog*] [*files*]
    stdin read if – or no *files* specified
Options:
      – f *pfile*   use *pfile* as program
      – F*c*   field separator character is *c*
      – v *var* =*val*
                assign *val* to **nawk** variable *var*

prog   program line (should be in single quotes)

Δ **NEQN** — **nroff** Compatible Math Formatter (See **EQN**)
% **neqn** [*options*] [*files*]
    stdin read if no *files* specified
Options:
      – d*xy*   set start delimiter to x and end delimeter to y
      – f*n*   set to font n
      – p*n*   set sub- and superscripts in point size n
      – s*n*   set in point size n
      – T*dev*   format for specified device

NET — Execute Command on Remote System (DEC only)
% **net** *remote* [*cmd* [*args*]]

    remote   format: *system_name channel_number*
    cmd   **/bin/sh – i** default

NEWFORM — Change Text File Format
% **newform** [– **s**] [*options*] [*files*]
    stdin read if no *files* specified
Options:
      – a*n*   append n characters to end of line
      – b*n*   truncate n characters from beginning
                of line
      – c*k*   set prefix/suffix character to k (space default)
      – e*n*   truncate n characters from end of line
      – f   write tab format before output (– **8** default)
      – i*format* set tab format (– **8** default)
      – l*n*   set line length to n characters (**72** default)
      – o*format* replace spaces by tabs according to
                tab format (– **8** default)
      – p*n*   prefix n characters to the beginning of line
      – s   remove characters before first tab,
                place up to 8 at the end of the line

NEWGRP — Login to New Group
% **newgrp** [*option*] [*group*]
    user's login group used if no *group* specified
Option:
      –   change environment as if user logged
                   in again

NEWS — Print News Items
% **news** [*options*] [*items*]
Options:
      – a   print all items
      – n   print names (not contents) of current items
      – s   print number of current items

NICE — Run Command at Low Priority
% nice [*option*] *command* [*args*]
   priority lowered by 10 if *option* not specified
Option:
   −*n*   lower scheduling priority by *n*, range **1–19**

NL — Line Numbering Filter
% nl [*options*] [*file*]
   stdin read if no *file* specified
Options:
   − **b***type*   number specified lines:
                  Types:
                  a   all lines
                  n   no lines
                  p*string* lines containing *string*
                  t   lines with text only (default)
   − **d***xx*   specify delimiters for start of logical page
                  section (\: default)
   − **f***type*   like − **b** except for footer (**n** default)
   − **h***type*   like − **b** except for header (**n** default)
   − **i***n*   page number increment (**1** default)
   − **l***n*   *n* blank lines treated as one (**1** default)
   − **n***format*   line numbering format:
                  ln left justify, zero suppressed
                  rn right justify, zero suppressed (default)
                  rz right justify, zero filled
   − **p**   don't restart numbers at logical page ends
   − **s***c*   use *c* between number and text (**tab** default)
   − **v***n*   number first page *n* (**1** default)
   − **w***n*   set size of number field (**6** default)

Θ **NM** — Print Symbol Table
% nm [*options*] *files*
Options:
   − **e**   print static and external symbols only
   − **f**   print full output, including redundant
                  symbols
   − **h**   don't print header
   − **l**   flag "weak" symbols with an *
   − **n**   sort external symbols by name
   − **o**   print value & size in octal (decimal default)
   − **p**   produce parsed output
   − **r**   print name of archive or object file
                  before each line
   − **T**   truncate symbol names to fit columns
   − **u**   print undefined symbols only
   − **v**   sort external symbols by value
   − **V**   print version information
   − **x**   print value & size in hexadecimal

NOHUP — Run Command Ignoring Hangups
% nohup *command* [*args*]

Δ **NON-BTL** — Reinstall **mm** without Bell Labs Features
% non-btl

NOTIFY — Notify User of New Mail
% **notify** [*option*]
Options:
    -n   turn off notify facility
    -y [**-m** *mfile*]
               turn on notify facility and optionally save
               new messages in *mfile* (**$HOME/.mailfile**
               default)

If no *option*, report notify status.

△ **NROFF** — Format Text (See **TROFF**)
% **nroff** [*options*] [*files*]
    stdin read if – or no *files* specified
Options:

-cname	prepend compacted files **/usr/lib/macros/[u]cmp.[nt.][dt.]**name
-e	equally space words in justified lines
-h	speed output with tabs (set every 8 spaces)
-i	read **stdin** after all *files*
-kname	compact macros used and place in [**dt**].name
-mname	prepend macro file **/usr/lib/tmac/tmac.**name
-nn	number first page *n*
-olist	print only listed page numbers
-q	invoke simultaneous input/output mode of **.rd**
-ran	set number register *a* to *n*
-s[n]	stop every n pages (**1** default)
-Tterm	specify output terminal (**lp**, **37**, **300**, **300s**, **382**, **450**, **832**, **2631**, **4000A**, **tn300**, and **X** supported)
-un	overstrike bold characters *n* times (**1** or **0** default)
-z	print only output from **.tm** requests
list	comma-separated, *n–m* means range, *–n* means beginning to page *n*, *n–* means page *n* to end

OD — File Dump
% **od** [*options*] [*file*] [[**+**]*offset*[*base*][**b**]]
    stdin read if no *file* specified
Options:

-b	byte dump in octal
-c	byte dump in ASCII characters
-d	word dump in unsigned decimal
-D	long word dump in unsigned decimal
-f	long word dump in floating point
-F	double long word dump in floating point
-o	word dump in octal (default)
-O	long word dump in octal
-s	word dump in signed decimal
-S	long word dump in signed decimal
-v	verbose output
-x	word dump in hexadecimal
-X	long word dump in hexadecimal

(continued)

OD, continued

offset	specify octal offset to start dumping *file*
+	required if *file* is omitted
b	indicate offset is in 512 byte blocks
base	base for offset and addresses (octal default)
	. decimal
	x hexadecimal

Δ **OSDD** — Print OSDD Format Documents (See **MM**)
% **osdd** [*options*] [*files*]
    option list printed if no arguments specified
Options:
– 12	use 12 pitch print
– c	invoke **col** (default except for fancy printers)
– e	invoke **neqn**
– E	invoke **– e** option of **nroff**
– t	invoke **tbl**
– T_term_	specify terminal type (**$TERM** default)
– y	use non-compacted macros

Any other options are passed to **nroff**.

PACK — Compress Files
% **pack** [*options*] *files*
files are compressed to *files*.**z**; originals removed
Options:
–	print statistical information on **stdout**
– f	force packing of *files*

PAGE — View File by Screenful or by Line (See **MORE**)
% **page** [*options*] *files*

PASSWD — Change Login Password
% **passwd** [*option*]
Option:
– s	display password attributes

PASTE — Horizontally Concatenate Files
% **paste** [*options*] *files*
    stdin read if **–** specified in *files*
Options:
– d_list_	use *list* chars as line separators (**tab** default)
– s	merge subsequent lines from one file
list	characters reused when exhausted

PCAT — Unpack and Concatenate Packed Files (See **PACK**)
% **pcat** *files*

Θ **PCC** — Portable C Compiler (See **CC**)
% **pcc** [*options*] *files*
Options:
– B_string_	substitute compiler passes
– c	suppress link edit; produce **.o** files
– D_name_[=_def_]	define *name* as *def* (**1** default)
– E	only preprocessor output to **stdout**
– f	use floating point software
– g	enable **sdb** debugger
– I_dir_	search *dir* before standard ones
– o *output*	specify output file (**a.out** default)
– O	optimize object code produced
– p	set up object files for profiling

(continued)

PCC, continued
-   **-P**   only preprocessor output to *files*.**i**
-   **-S**   put assembler source in *files*.**s**
-   **-t**[*passes*] indicate which passes to substitute
-   **-U***symb*   remove initial definition of *symb*
-   **-W***pass, arg1* [*args*]

                        give arguments to *pass*
                        args is comma-separated list
                        pass   one or more of **p02bal**
                             p   preprocessor
                             0   compiler
                             2   optimizer
                             b   basic block analyzer
                             a   assembler
                             l   link editor

PDP11 — True Exit Status if PDP-11
% **pdp11**

PG — View File by Screenful (See **MORE**)
% **pg** [*options*] [*files*]
Options:
-   **+** /*pattern*/   start at first line containing *pattern*
-   **+***n*   start at line *n*
-   **-***n*   window is *n* lines
-   **-c**   clear screen for each page
-   **-e**   don't pause at end of file
-   **-f**   don't split long lines
-   **-n**   don't need newline after command letters
-   **-p** *prompt* set prompt to *prompt* (: default)
                        %d specifies page number
-   **-r**   restricted mode – disable shell escape
-   **-s**   print messages and prompts in reverse video

Enter **h** to display a list of commands.

Δ **PIC** — **troff** Preprocessor for Drawing Pictures
% **pic** [*option*] *file*
Option:
-   **-T***dev*   specify device

POSTDAISY — Diablo 630 to PostScript Translator
% **postdaisy** [*options*] [*file*]
Option:
-   **-c** *n*   make *n* copies of each page
-   **-f** *fname*   use font *fname* (**Courier** default)
-   **-h** *hmi*   horizontal motion index (**12** default)
-   **-m** *n*   magnification factor (**1.0** default)
-   **-n** *n*   number of logical pages per physical page
                        (**1** default)
-   **-o** *list*   print only specified pages; ranges or
                        comma-separated list
-   **-p** *mode*   **portrait** or **landscape** mode (**portrait** default)
-   **-r** *lflag*   linefeed/carriage return behavior
                        1   linefeed generates carriage return
                        2   carriage return generates linefeed
                        3   both **1** and **2**
-   **-s** *size*   set point size to *size*
-   **-v** *vmi*   vertical motion index (**8** default)
-   **-x** *xoff*   origin offset; positive means right
                        (**0.25** inches default)
-   **-y** *yoff*   origin offset; positive means up
                        (**0.25** inches default)

POSTDMD — DMD Bitmap to Postscript
% **postdmd** [*options*] [*files*]
    stdin read if – or no *files* specified
Options:
–b *n*	pack using *n*-byte patterns (**6** default)
–c *n*	make *n* copies of each page
–f	flip sense of bits before printing
–m *n*	magnification factor (**1.0** default)
–n *n*	number of logical pages per physical page (**1** default)
–o *list*	print only specified pages; ranges or comma-separated list
–p *mode*	**portrait** or **landscape** mode (**portrait** default)
–x *xoff*	origin offset; positive means right (**0** inches default)
–y *yoff*	origin offset; positive means up (**0** inches default)

POSTIO — Serial Interface to PostScript Printer
% **postio** –l *line* [*options*] [*files*]
    stdin read if – or no *files* specified
Options:
–b *rate*	set specified baud rate (**9600** default)
–B *size*	set buffer size (**2048** bytes default)
–D	debug; log everything to **stderr**
–i	run in interactive mode (non-spool use)
–L *log*	log received data in *log* (**stdout** default)
–P *str*	send *str* to printer before printing
–q	disable status queries
–R *n*	run characteristics of **postio**
	1 single process (default)
	2 separate read and write processes
–S	slow mode (not recommended)
–t	write received data to **stdout** (non-spool use)
line	communications line to use

POSTMD — Matrix to PostScript Printer
% **postmd** [*options*] [*files*]
    stdin read if – or no *files* specified
Options:
–b *n*	pack using *n*-byte patterns (**6** default)
–c *n*	make *n* copies of each page
–d *msize*	matrix dimensions; either *msize* or *ysize***x***xsize*
–g *list*	gray scale list; 255=white, 0=black
–i *list*	real number line partition list for gray scale assignment (**-1,0,1** default)
–m *n*	magnification factor (**1.0** default)
–n *n*	number of logical pages per physical page (**1** default)
–o *list*	print only specified pages; ranges or comma-separated list
–p *mode*	**portrait** or **landscape** mode (**portrait** default)
–w *y1,x1,y2,x2*	upper left and lower right of sub-matrix
–x *xoff*	origin offset; positive means right (**0** inches default)
–y *yoff*	origin offset; positive means up (**0** inches default)

POSTPLOT — Plot(4) to PostScript Translator
% **postplot** [*options*] [*files*]
    stdin read if – or no *files* specified
Options:
– **c** *n*	make *n* copies of each page
– **f** *font*	print text in *font* (**Courier** default)
– **m** *n*	magnification factor (**1.0** default)
– **n** *n*	number of logical pages per physical page (**1** default)
– **o** *list*	print only specified pages; ranges or comma-separated list
– **p** *mode*	**portrait** or **landscape** mode (**landscape** default)
– **w** *n*	set line width to *n* points (**0** default)
– **x** *xoff*	origin offset; positive means right (**0** inches default)
– **y** *yoff*	origin offset; positive means up (**0** inches default)

POSTPRINT — Text to PostScript Translator
% **postprint** [*options*] [*files*]
    stdin read if – or no *files* specified
Options:
– **c** *n*	make *n* copies of each page
– **f** *font*	print text in *font* (**Courier** default)
– **l** *n*	set page length to *n* lines (**66** default)
– **m** *n*	magnification factor (**1.0** default)
– **n** *n*	number of logical pages per physical page (**1** default)
– **o** *list*	print only specified pages; ranges or comma-separated list
– **p** *mode*	**portrait** or **landscape** mode (**portrait** default)
– **r** *lflag*	linefeed/carriage return behavior
	0 ignore carriage returns (default)
	1 just do carriage return
	2 carriage return generates linefeed
– **s** *size*	set point size to *size*
– **t** *n*	set tabs every *n* columns (**8** default)
– **x** *xoff*	origin offset; positive means right (**0.25** inches default)
– **y** *yoff*	origin offset; positive means up (**0.25** inches default)

POSTREVERSE — Reverse PostScript Page Order
% **/usr/lib/lp/postscript/postreverse** [*options*] [*file*]
    stdin read if no *file* specified
Options:
– **o** *list*	print only specified pages; ranges or comma-separated list
– **r**	don't reverse; just reformat comments

POSTTEK — Tektronix 4014 to PostScript Translator
% **/usr/lib/lp/postscript/posttek** [*options*] [*files*]
    stdin read if – or no *files* specified
Options:
– **c** *n*	make *n* copies of each page (**1** default)
– **f** *font*	print text in *font* (**Courier** default)
– **m** *n*	magnification factor (**1.0** default)
– **n** *n*	number of logical pages per physical page (**1** default)
– **o** *list*	print only specified pages; ranges or comma-separated list

(continued)

−p *mode*	**portrait** or **landscape** mode (**landscape** default)
−w *n*	set line width to *n* points (**0** default)
−x *xoff*	origin offset; positive means right (**0** inches default)
−y *yoff*	origin offset; positive means up (**0** inches default)

PR — Print Files

% **pr** [*options*] [*files*]

    stdin read if − or no *files* specified

Options:

+*n*	begin printing at page *n* (**1** default)
−*n*	produce *n* column output (**1** default)
−a	print multi-column output across page
−d	print double spaced
−e*cn*	expand input tabs to every *n*th position using *c* as tab char (*n*=**8** default; *c*=**tab** default)
−f	use form feed character for new page, pause before first page if **stdout** is to terminal
−F	fold input lines to fit
−h *head*	use *head* as heading line (file name default)
−i*cn*	convert whitespace to tabs every *n*th position *c* as tab char (*n*=**8** default; *c*=**tab** default)
−l*n*	set page length to *n* lines (**66** default)
−m	merge and print all *files*, one per column
−n*cn*	number lines with *n*-wide numbers followed by *c* (*n*=**5** default; *c*=**tab** default)
−o*n*	set line offset to *n* (**0** default)
−p	pause between pages if output is to a terminal
−r	no error messages if *files* cannot be opened
−s*c*	set column separator to *c* (**tab** default)
−t	don't print page heading or trailing lines
−w*n*	set line width to *n* (**72** default for equal width multi-column output, no limit otherwise)

PRINTF — Formatted Print

% **printf** *format* [*args*]

format consists of:

    characters copied to the output

    %s specifiers for string converson

    %% which prints as %

    C-language escape sequences

args are strings to be formatted and printed

PRIOCNTL — Process Scheduler Control

% **priocntl** **−l**

    display class configuration information

% **priocntl** **−d** [**−i** *type*] [*idlist*]

    display scheduling information about specified processes

% **priocntl** **−e** [**−c** *class*] [*classopt*] *command* [*args*]

    execute *command* with specified priority

% **priocntl** **−s** [**−c** *class*] [*classopt*] [**−i** *type*] [*list*]

    set scheduling priority of specified processes

(continued)

Options:

- **-c** *class*   class of processes; if not specified
      must select processes all in one class
      RT   real time
      TS   time sharing
- **-i** *type*   process type (**pid** default)
      all   all processes
      class   **RT** or **TS** in *idlist*
            defaults to **-c** class or class of
            selected process's current class
      gid   *idlist* contains group IDs
      pgid   *idlist* contains process group IDs
      pid   *idlist* contains process IDs
      ppid   *idlist* contains parent process IDs
      sid   *idlist* contains session IDs
      uid   *idlist* contains effective user IDs

idlist   list of IDs of type specified by **-i** option
      default is related ID of **priocntl** command itself

class_opt   class specific options

- **-m** *lim*   set user priority limit to *lim* (TS only)
- **-p** *pri*   set processes' priority to *pri*
- **-t** *quan* [**-r** *res*]
      set time quantum to *quan*
      res is fraction of second resolution
      (**1000** default)

Θ PROF — Display Profile Data

% prof [*options*] [*file*]

    a.out used if no *file* specified

Options:

- **-a**   sort by increasing symbol address
- **-c**   sort by decreasing number of calls
- **-g**   include static functions
- **-h**   don't print report heading
- **-l**   don't include static functions (default)
- **-m** *profile*   name of profile data source (**mon.out** default)
- **-n**   sort lexically by symbol name
- **-o**   print symbol address in octal with name
- **-s**   print summary on **stderr**
- **-t**   sort by decreasing percentage of
      total time (default)
- **-V**   print version information
- **-x**   print symbol address in hex with name
- **-z**   include symbols even if zero calls and time

Θ PRS — Print Parts of SCCS Files

% prs [*options*] *files*

    SCCS filenames read from **stdin** if *files* is −

Options:

- **-a**   include removed deltas
- **-c**[*date*]   cutoff date and time in format
      YY[*MM*[*DD*[*HH*[*MM*[*SS*]]]]]
- **-d**[*text*]   output specification (includes data keys)
- **-e**   include deltas at *sid* or *date* and earlier
      (see **-c** or **-r**)
- **-l**   include deltas at *sid* or *date* and later
      (see **-c** or **-r**)
- **-r**[*sid*]   specify SCCS ID of version (top delta default)

PS — Report Process Status
% **ps** [*options*]
Options:

– a	print all processes **except** session leaders and non-terminal associated
– c	include scheduler priorities
– d	print all processes except group leaders
– e	print all processes
– f	print full listing
– g *list*	list only processes whose leaders are in *list*
– j	print session & process group ID
– l	long listing (more info than **– f**)
– n *list*	use *list* for namelist (/unix default)
– p *list*	list only processes whose IDs are in *list*
– s *list*	list info about session leaders in *list*
– t *list*	list only processes of terminals in *list*
– u *list*	list only processes with user IDs in *list*
list	comma or blank-separated list with optional enclosing double quotes

Δ **PTX** — Permuted Index
% **ptx** [*options*] [*input*[*output*]]
    stdin and **stdout** used if *input* or *output* not specified
Option:

– b *file*	use characters in *file* to separate words (**tab**, **\n** and **space** are default separators)
– f	sort upper and lower case together
– g *n*	set gap between output parts to *n* characters (**3** default)
– i *file*	don't use words in *file* as keywords; if neither **– i** or **– o** are used, **/usr/lib/eign** is used as *file*
– o *file*	use only words in *file* as keys
– r	treat leading characters as reference ID
– t	prepare ouput for **troff** (**nroff** default)
– w *n*	set length of output line to *n* (**72** default for nroff, **100** for **troff**)

PWD — Print Working Directory Name
% **pwd**

Θ **RATFOR** — Rational FORTRAN Translator
% **ratfor** [*options*] [*files*]
Options:

– 6*c*	make continuation char *c* and put in column 6 (**&** in column **1** default)
– C	copy comments to output
– h	make quoted strings into **27H** constructs

RCP — Remote File Copy
% **rcp** [*option*] *file1 file2*
    copy from *file1* to *file2*
Option:

– p	attempt to preserve modify and access times

% **rcp** [*options*] *files dir*
    copy *files* to directory *dir*
Options:

– p	attempt to preserve modify and access times
– r	copy each subtree rooted at *file*

RED — Restricted Version of **ed** Text Editor
% **red** [*options*] [*file*]
Options:
    –C   work with encrypted file (simulate C cmd)
    –p *string* specify prompt string
    –s   suppress counts, diagnostics, etc.
    –x   work with encrypted file (simulate X cmd)

Θ **REGCMP** — Compile Regular Expression
% **regcmp** [*option*] *files*
    compile **regular expression** in *file* into *file*.**i**
Option:
    –   place output in *file*.**c** instead of *file*.**i**

RELOGIN — Log In to Current Layer
% **/usr/bin/layersys/relogin** [*option*] *line*
Option:
    –s   suppress error messages
    line   **utmp** entry to change

RJESTAT — Report RJE Status, Simulate IBM Console
% **rjestat** [*ibms*] [**–s***ibm*] [**–c***ibm cmds*]
Options:
    –c*ibm cmd* interpret *cmd* as if in remote console mode
    –j*ibm job* report on status of *job* on *ibm*
    –s*ibm*   begin interactive status console to *ibm* after
                  processing arguments

    ibm host name (from **/usr/rje/***lines*) to report on

RKSH — Restricted Korn Shell (See **KSH**)
% **rksh** [*options*] [*args*]

RLOGIN — Remote Login
% **rlogin** [*options*] *hostname*
Options:
    –8   use 8-bit data
    –e *c*   set escape character to *c* (~ default)
    –l *user* use *user* as remote login name
    –L   allow session to run in litout mode

RM — Remove Files
% **rm** [*options*] *files*
Options:
    –f   force removal of files without write
              permission
    –i   ask for confirmation before each delete
    –r   recursively delete directories

Θ **RMDEL** — Remove an SCCS Delta Version
% **rmdel –r***sid files*
    SCCS filenames read from **stdin** if *files* is **–**
Option:
    –r*sid*   specify SCCS ID of version to be removed

RMDIR — Remove Empty Directories (See **RM**)
% **rmdir** [*options*] *directories*
Options:
    –p   remove empty parent directories
    –s   suppress error messages

RSH — Remote Shell
% **rsh** [*options*] *hostname* [*command*]
% **rsh** *hostname* [*options*] [*command*]
% *hostname* [*options*] [*command*]
Options:
−l *user*	use *user* as the remote username (local user name default)
−n	redirect input of **rsh** from **/dev/null**

If **rsh** is invoked by any name other than **rsh** it assumes
the invocation name is a hostname.

RUPTIME — Report Status of Local Machines
% **ruptime** [*options*]
Options:
−a	include idle users in count
−l	sort by load average
−r	reverse sort order
−t	sort by uptime
−u	sort by number of users

RWHO — Who is On Local Machines
% **rwho** [*option*]
Option:
−a	include idle users in count

Θ **SACT** — Print SCCS File Editing Activity
% **sact** *files*
  SCCS filenames read from **stdin** if files is −

SAG — System Activity Graph
% **sag** [*options*]
Options:
−e *time*	end time of sample (**18:00** default)
−f *file*	read input from *file* (**/var/adm/sa/sa***dd* default, *dd* is current day)
−i *sec*	use *sec* second intervals
−s *time*	start time of sample (**08:00** default)
−T *term*	format output for terminal *term* (**$TERM** default)
−x *spec*	specifications for x axis
−y *spec*	specifications for y axis

time is in form *hh*[:*mm*]

SAR — System Activity Report
% **sar** [*data_options*] [**−o** *file*] *t* [*n*]
  sample current system activity counters
% **sar** [*data_options*] [**−s** *start*] [**−e** *end*] [**−i** *sec*] [**−f** *file*]
  extract system information from previously stored file
Data Options:
−a	file access routines
−A	all reports
−b	buffer activity
−c	system calls
−C	Remote File Sharing data caching
−d	block device activity
−D	Remote File Sharing activity
−g	paging activity; page stealing daemon
−k	kernel memory allocation activities
−m	message and semaphore activity

(continued)

SAR, continued
-p	paging activity and page faults
-q	queue activity
-r	unused memory and disk blocks
-S	server and request queue status
-u	cpu utilization (default)
-v	process, i-node and file table status
-w	system swapping and switching
-x	remote file sharing operations
-y	tty device activity

Options:
-e *end*	ending time of report (*hh*[:*mm*[:*ss*]])
-f *file*	extract information from *file* (**/var/adm/sa/sa***dd* default, *dd* is current day)
-i *n*	sample report every *n* seconds (all intervals in data file default)
-o *file*	save samples in binary format in *file*
-s *start*	starting time of report (*hh*[:*mm*[:*ss*]])

n   sample system for *n* intervals (**1** default)
t   each system sample *t* seconds long

Θ **SCC** — C Compiler to Generate Stand-Alone Programs
% **scc** [*lib*] [*options*] [*files*]
lib can be one of the following:
+	don't load configuration library
+A	load RP04/05/06 and TU16 library (default)
+B	load RK11/05, RP11/03 and TM11/TU16 library

Options:
-B*string*	substitute compiler passes
-c	suppress link edit; produce **.o** files
-D*name*[*=def*]	define *name* as *def* (**1** default)
-E	only preprocessor output to **stdout**
-f	use floating point software
-g	enable **sdb** debugger (VAX only)
-l*dir*	search *dir* before standard ones
-o *output*	name of output file (**a.out** default)
-O	optimize object code produced
-p	set up object files for profiling
-P	only preprocessor output to *files***.i**
-S	only assembler source to *files***.s**
-t[*passes*]	indicate which passes to substitute
-U*symb*	remove initial definition of *symb*
-W*pass*, *arg1*[*,args*]	
-d*n*	offset *n* bytes for externals
pass	one or more of **p012al**

Θ **SCCS** — Source Code Control System
See **ADMIN**, **CDC**, **COMB**, **DELTA**, **GET**, **PRS**, **RMDEL**, **SACT**, **SCCSDIFF**, **UNGET**, **VAL**, and **WHAT**

Θ **SCCSDIFF** — SCCS Version Difference
% **sccsdiff** **-r***sid1* **-r***sid2* [*options*] *files*
Options:
-p	format output using **pr**
-s*n*	file segment size of *n*

SCRIPT — Make Log Of Terminal Session
% **script** [*option*] [*file*]
Options:
    –a   append to logfile

default log file is **typescript**

Θ **SDB** — Symbolic Debugger for C & F77
% **sdb** [*options*] [*objfile* [*corefile* [*dirs*]]]
Options:
    –e   ignore symbolic information
    –s *n*   don't stop process that receives signal *n*;
              –s option can be used multiple times
    –V   print version information
    –w   overwriting locations in files permitted
    –W   suppress warnings

objfile   executable file compiled with **–g** option
              (**a.out** default)
corefile   core image dump file; – causes all core image
              files to be ignored (**core** default)
dirs   default location for source files

Addresses:
    proc : *variable* [*,num*]
    proc   current procedure default
    num   optional occurrence on stack, most current
              first
    [*m;n*]   range of subscripts (* indicates all)
    file: *n*   (or *proc* :*n*) line within a file

Commands (for data):
    n ?*lf*   show value at line *n* in format *lf* (**i** default)
    n =[*lf*]   show address at line *n* in format *lf* (**lx** default)
    t   show stack trace
    T   show top line of stack trace
    var :?*lf*   show contents of *var* in format *lf* (**i** default)
    var =[*lf*] show address of *var* in format *lf* (**lx** default)
    var / [*nlf*] show contents of *var*, length *l* in format *f*;
              show region of memory of *n* units of length *l*
    var ! *value* set *var* to *value*
    x   show registers and current instruction
    X   show current machine instruction

Formats:
    l   length specifier (use with format **cduox** only):
              byte, **h**alf word, **l**ong word
    f   format: **c**haracter, **d**ecimal, **u**nsigned, **o**ctal,
              he**x**adecimal, **f**loating point (32 bit), **g**
              floating point (64 bit), **s**tring pointer, **a**ddress
              of *var*, **p**ointer to procedures, machine
              language **i**nstruction with numeric and
              symbolic addresses, machine **I**nstruction
              with numeric addresses only

Commands (for source files);
    inc +   advance current line by *inc* lines, print line
    inc –   go back *inc* lines, print line
    n   set current line to *n*, print line
    /*re*/   search forward for line containing *re*
    ?*re*?   search backward for line containing *re*
    e *dir*   look in *dir* for source files (current default)
    e *file*   set current file to *file*

(continued)

SDB, continued

e *proc*	set current file to file containing *proc*
p	print current line
w	show 10 lines around the current line
z	print current line plus next 9 lines

(*inc* specifies number of breakpoints to ignore)

Commands (for execution of source program):

addr **:m** *inc*	single step until specified location is modified
proc (*args*)	run named procedure with *args*
proc (*args*) **/m**	run named procedure, show returned value in format *m* (**d** is default format)
n **a**	announce: if *n* is of form *proc* :, print top level of stack, else print last executed line
n **b** [*cmds*]	set breakpoint at line *n*; if no *cmds*, stop before breakpoint; otherwise execute *cmds* when breakpoint is reached *cmds* semicolon-separated list
B	show currently active breakpoints
n **c** [*inc*]	continue after breakpoint or interrupt; ignore signal; ignore *inc* – 1 breakpoints
n **C** [*inc*]	continue after breakpoint or interrupt; reactivate signal; ignore *inc* – 1 breakpoints
[*n*] **d**	delete breakpoint at line *n*; if no *n*, interactive delete
D	delete all breakpoints
n **g** [*inc*]	continue after breakpoint, resume at line *n*;
i[*cnt*]	single step *cnt* instructions (**1** default); ignore signal
I[*cnt*]	single step *cnt* instructions; reactivate signal
k	stop program that is being debugged
l	display last executed line
var **$m** *inc*	single step until specified location is modified
[*l*] **v**	toggle verbose mode (with **sSm**); if no *l*, show changed source file and/or subroutine names; *l* if ≥1, show source line before executing if ≥2, also print assembler statements
[*inc*] **r** [*args*]	if no *args*, reuse previous *args*; otherwise run program with *args*; if *args* begins with > redirect **stdout**, if <, **stdin**
[*inc*] **R**	run program with no *args*
s [*inc*]	single step through *inc* lines; if no *inc*, run one line of program
S [*inc*]	like **s**, except step through procedure calls

Miscellaneous Commands:

#	comment
!*command*	pass *command* to **sh**
" *string* **"**	print *string*
< *file*	read commands from *file*
^D	show next 10 lines: instructions, source or data
M	display address maps
M [**?/**] [*****] *b e f*	enter new values for address map **?** text map

/	data map
*	modify second segment
b	beginning
e	end
f	file offset
newline	display next source line or memory location
q	exit debugger

Debugging Commands:

Q	list procedures and files being debugged
V	display version number
Y	toggle debugger

SDIFF — Side-By-Side Difference
% **sdiff** [*options*] *file1 file2*
Options:

−l	print only identical lines on left side
−o *file*	merge *file1* and *file2* to *file*, identical lines are passed directly, else user prompted:
e	edit an empty file
e b	edit both left and right columns
e l	edit left column
e r	edit right column
l	append left column
q	exit
r	append right column
s	suppress printing of identical lines
v	enable printing of identical lines
−s	suppress printing of identical lines
−w *n*	set width of output line to *n* (**130** default)

SE — Screen Editor
% **se** [*options*] [*file*]
Options:

−i *file*	read **se** commands from *file*
−o *file*	copy commands from this invocation of **se** into *file*
−s	limit number of status messages printed
−T[*term*]	set terminal time to *term* (**$SETERM** or **$TERM** default); if no *term*, all known terminals listed

SED — Stream Editor
% **sed** [*options*] [*files*]
    stdin read if no *files* specified
Options:

−e *script*	editor commands in *script* executed
−f *file*	editor commands read from *file*
−n	suppress unrequested output

Command Format:
    [*addr1* [,*addr2*]] *function* [*args*]
Addresses:

.	current line
$	last line
n	*n*th line
/*re*/	next line with /*re*/
\c*re*c	as above using *c* as delimiter
\n	matches newline embedded in pattern space
	no specified address matches all lines
	one address matches only matching lines
	two addresses select inclusive range

e regular expression

See Page 88 for Regular Expressions.

Commands (number in ( ) is number of addresses; the number and () should not be entered):

(0)	empty commands are ignored
(0)#	if # is first character, treat entire line as comment
(2)! *func*	apply *func* to addresses not selected
(0): *label*	label for **b** and **t** commands
(1)=	write current line number to **stdout**
(2){	execute commands through } if pattern space is selected
(1)**a**\[**ENTER**]*text*	append; end with period alone on a line
(2)**b** *label*	branch :*label*
(2)**c**\[**ENTER**]*text*	change pattern space
(2)**d**	delete pattern space
(2)**D**	delete first line of pattern space
(2)**g**	replace pattern space with hold space
(2)**G**	append pattern space to hold space
(2)**h**	replace hold space with pattern space
(2)**H**	append hold space to pattern space
(1)**i**\[**ENTER**]*text*	insert *text* before current line
(2)**l**	list pattern space on **stdout**; "spells out" control characters
(2)**n**	copy pattern space to **stdout**
(2)**N**	append next input line to pattern space with embedded newline
(2)**p**	print pattern space on **stdout**
(2)**P**	print first line of pattern space on **stdout**
(1)**q**	quit by branching to end of script
(1)**r** *file*	read contents of *file*
(2)**s**/*re*/*nre*/*flgs*	substitute *nre* for *re*

flgs are:

n	substitute in just *n* occurrence
g	globally (non-overlapping)
p	print pattern space if replacement was made
w *file*	write pattern space to *file* if replacement was made

(2)**t** *label*	branch to :*label* if substitutions made
(2)**w** *file*	write pattern space to *file*
(2)**x**	exchange pattern and hold space
(2)**y**/*str1*/*str2*/	replace *str1* with *str2*; strings must be of equal length

SH — Bourne Shell (See Pages 84-87)

% **sh** [*options*] [*args*]

Options:

− −	don't change any flags (useful to set **$1** to −)
− **a**	mark modified export variables
− **c** *cmd*	execute *cmd* (default reads commands from file named in first entry of *args*)
− **e**	if non-interactive, exit if a command fails
− **f**	disable wildcarding

(continued)

−h	locate and remember functions on definition instead of on execution
−i	set interactive mode
−k	all keyword arguments placed in environment
−n	read commands without executing them
−p	don't set effective IDs to real IDs
−r	set restricted mode
−s	read commands from **stdin**
−t	read and execute one command, then exit
−u	set error upon substituting an unset variable
−v	print input lines as read
−x	print commands, as executed, with arguments

SHL — Manage Shell Layers
% **shl**

Θ **SIZE** — Size of Object File
% **size** [*options*] [*files*]
    a.out read if no *files* specified
Options:

−f	include details on each section
−F	include details on each segment
−n	include data on non-loadable segments or non-allocatable sections
−o	print number in octal (decimal default)
−V	print **size** version number on **stderr**
−x	print number in hexadecimal

SLEEP — Suspend Execution for Specified Duration
% **sleep** *seconds*

Θ **SNO** — Snobol Interpreter
% **sno** [*files*]
    stdin read after *files*

SORT — Sort/Merge Files
% **sort** [*options*] [*files*]
    stdin read if − or no *files* specified
Options:

    +*pos1* [**−***pos2*]

> sort only from *pos1* to *pos2*; if *pos2* not specified, key includes up to the end of line; *pos1* and *pos2* of the form: $m[.n][$**bdfiMnr**$])$
>
> | | |
> |---|---|
> | *m* | *m* fields from start of line skipped (**0** default) |
> | *n* | *n* characters from start of field skipped (**0** default) |
>
> **bdfiMnr**
> > option applies only to specified key

−b	ignore leading tabs and spaces
−c	check that input is in sorted order
−d	dictionary order (use only letters, digits, tabs, and spaces)
−f	sort upper case and lower case together
−i	ignore non-printables in comparisons
−m	merge already sorted *files*
−M	compare as months (implies **−b**)
−n	numeric sort (implies **−b**)
−o *output*	place sorted results in *output*

SORT, continued
    −**r**   reverse sort; descending order
    −**t**c   set field separator to c (**tab** default)
    −**u**   output only one occurrence of duplicate lines
    −**y**[*mem*]   kbytes of memory to start with,
                    0 = minimum, no arg = maximum
    −**z**[*size*] bytes in longest line read

Δ **SPELL** — Find Spelling Errors
% **spell** [*options*] [*files*]
    stdin read if no *files* specified
Options:
    +*local*   remove all words found in *local* from output
    −**b**   check British spelling
    −**l**   run **spell** on all included files
    −**v**   print words not literally in dictionary and
                    derivations
    −**x**   print stems for each word

SPLIT — Break File into Pieces
% **split** [*option*] [*file* [*name*]]
    stdin read if − or no *file* specified
Options:
    −*n*   set size of split files to *n* lines (**1000** default)
    name   output *name***aa**, *name***ab**, ... (**xaa** default)

SRCHTXT — Search Message Data Bases
% **srchtxt** [*options*] [*text*]
Options:
    −**l** *locale*   access files in
                      /usr/lib/locale/*locale***/LC_MESSAGES**
    −**m** *msgfile*
                      access specified *msgfile* which can be
                      a comma-delimited list. Leading /
                      indicates pathname, else assume directory
                      /usr/lib/locale/*locale***/LC_MESSAGES**
    −**s**   suppress printing of message numbers

text   string or regular expression to be searched for

If not otherwise specified, *locale* is determined by the value of
the **$LC_MESSAGES** or the **$LANG** environment variable.

STARTER — Help for Beginners
% **starter**

STRCHG — Change Streams Configuration
% **strchg** −**h** *module1*[,*module2* ...]
    push modules onto stream
% **strchg** −**f** *file*
    configure stream with modules specified in *file*
% **strchg** −**p** [*options*]
    pop module from stream
Options:
    −**a**   pop all modules above topmost driver
    −**u** *module*   pop all modules above *module*

STRCONF — Print List of Modules in a Stream
% **strconf** [*option*]
Options:
  – m *module*
               determine if *module* is in stream
  –t   print name of topmost module only

STRINGS — Search Binary Files for ASCII Strings
% **strings** [*options*] *files*
Options:
  – a   search beyond initialized data space
  –n *n*   use *n* as minimum string length (**4** default)
  –o   print octal offset in file for each string

Θ **STRIP** — Remove Symbol Table and Relocation Bits
% **strip** [*options*] *files*
Options:
  –l   strip line number info only
  – r   reset relocation indexes in symbol table
  – s   reset line number indexes in symbol table
  – V   print version information
  – x   don't strip external or static symbol info

STTY — Set Terminal Options
% **stty** [– **a**] [– **g**] [*options*]
Options:
  – a   print all option settings
  – g   print settings in **stty** argument format

  n   set terminal baud rate to *n*
  term   set all modes for the specified terminal,
               term (**tty33**, **tty37**, **vt05**, **tn300**, **ti700**,
               and **tek** allowed)
  0   hang up phone line
  async   set normal async mode with clock modes
               xcibrg, **rcibrg**, **tsetcoff** and **rsetcoff**
  [–]**brkint** [do not] send **INTR** signal on input break
  bsn   set output delay after backspace (**0** or **1**)
  [–]**cdxon** [disable]/enable CD output flow control
  [–]**clocal** [enable]/disable modem control
  columns *n*
               set window to *n* columns
  cooked   disable raw input & output (same as – **raw**)
  [–]**cread** [disable]/enable receiver
  crn   set output delay after carriage return (**0** to **3**)
  csn   set character size to *n* bits (**5** to **8**)
  [–]**cstopb** set [one]/two stop bits per character
  ctab *c*   set CTAB char to *c* (used with **–stappl**)
  [–]**ctsxon** [disable]/enable CTS output flow control
  discard *c* set "discard output" character to *c*
               (ˆ**O** default)
  dsusp *c*   generate SIGTSTP signal when foreground
               process group attempts to read *c* (ˆ**Y**
               default)
  [–]**dtrxoff** [disable]/enable DTR input flow control
  [–]**echo**   [do not] echo all input characters
  [–]**echoctl** [do not] echo control chars as ˆ*char*
  [–]**echoe** [do not] echo **ERASE** for CRTs
  [–]**echok** [do not] echo a newline after **KILL**
  [–]**echoke** [do not] BS-SP-BS erase line on line kill
  [–]**echonl** [do not] echo newlines
  [–]**echoprt** [do not] echo erase char as char is "erased"

ek	reset **ERASE** to # and **KILL** to @
eof *c*	set end of file character to *c* (`^D` default)
eol *c*	set line delimiter to *c* (**NULL** default)
eol2 *c*	set additional line delimiter to *c*
erase *c*	set character **ERASE** character to *c* (# default)
[–]**evenp**	same as [–]**parenb** and **cs[8]**/7
ff*n*	set output delay after form-feed (**0** or **1**)
[–]**flusho**	[do not]/flush output buffers
[–]**hup**	[do not]/do hang up on last close
[–]**hupcl**	same as **hup**
[–]**icanon**	[disable]/enable checking for **ERASE** and **KILL**
[–]**icrnl**	[do not] map CR to NL on input
[–]**iexten**	[disable]/enable extended input functions
[–]**ignbrk**	[do not] ignore break on input
[–]**igncr**	[do not] ignore CR on input
[–]**ignpar**	[do not] ignore parity errors
[–]**imaxbel**	[do not] echo BEL when input too long
[–]**inlcr**	[do not] map input newline to carriage return
[–]**inpck**	[disable]/enable input parity check
intr *c*	set **INTR** (interrupt) character to *c* (DEL default)
[–]**isig**	[disable]/enable checking for **INTR**, **SWTCH** and **QUIT**
ispeed *n*	set input baud rate to *n* (**0** indicates **ispeed** is to be set to **ospeed**
[–]**istrip**	[do not] strip 8th bit of input characters
[–]**isxoff**	[disable]/enable isochronous input flow control
[–]**iuclc**	[do not] map input upper case to lower case
[–]**ixany**	allow [**XON**]/any character to restart **XOFF**
[–]**ixoff**	[disable]/enable **XON/XOFF** during input
[–]**ixon**	[disable]/enable **XON/XOFF** protocol
kill *c*	set line **KILL** character to *c* (@ default)
[–]**lcase**	same as [–]**xcase**, [–]**iuclc**, and [–]**olcuc**
[–]**LCASE**	same as [–]**lcase**
line *n*	set line discipline to *n* (**1** to **126** allowed)
lnext *c*	use *c* to escape special meaning of next char (`^V` default)
[–]**loblk**	[do not] block input from non-current layer
min *c*	set **MIN** value to *c* (used with – **icanon**)
[–]**markp**	[disable]/enable **parenb**, **cs7**/[**cs8**], **parodd** and **parext**
[–]**nl**	same as [**icrnl**]/– **icrnl** and [**onlcr**]/– **onlcr** [and – **inlcr**, – **igncr**, – **ocrnl**, and – **onlret**]
nl*n*	set output delay after newline (**0** or **1**)
[–]**noflsh**	[do not] no flush after **INTR** or **QUIT** or **SWTCH**
[–]**ocrnl**	[do not] map output carriage return to newline
[–]**oddp**	same as [–]**parenb**, [–]**parodd**, and **cs[8]**/7
[–]**ofdel**	set fill character to [**NUL**]/DEL
[–]**ofill**	delay output with [timing]/fill characters
[–]**olcuc**	[do not] map output lower case to upper case
[–]**onlcr**	[do not] map output newline to carriage return

[–]**onlret**	terminal does [not] carriage return after newline
[–]**onocr**	[do]/don't output carriage return at column 0
[–]**opost**	[do not] post-process output
ospeed n	set output baud rate to n (**0** causes an immediate hangup)
[–]**parenb**	[disable]/enable parity detection & generation
[–]**parext**	[disable]/enable checking for mark and space parity
[–]**parity**	same as [–]**parenb** and **cs**[**8**]/**7**
[–]**parmrk**	[do not] mark parity errors
[–]**parodd**	select [even]/odd parity
[–]**pendin**	[do not] retype pending input at next read
quit c	set **QUIT** character to c (ˆl default)
[–]**raw**	[disable]/enable raw input and output
rcibrg	use internal baud generator for rec clock
rcrset	use EIA-232-D pin 17 as xmit clock
rctset	use EIA-232-D pin 15 as xmit clock
reprint c	c will cause all unread characters to be reprinted (ˆR default)
rows n	set window size to n rows
rsetcoff	rec clock not provided
rsetcrbrg	output rec baud rate generator on CCITT V.24, ckt. 128
rsetctbrg	output xmit baud rate generator on CCITT V.24, ckt. 128
rsetcrset	output RC on CCITT V.24, ckt. 128
rsetctset	output TC on CCITT V.24, ckt. 128
[–]**rtsxoff**	[disable]/enable RTS input flow control
sane	reset all modes to "sane" values
[–]**spacep**	[disable]/enable **parenb**, **cs7** and **parext**
[–]**stappl**	use application/[line] mode on sync. line
start c	use c to resume output (ˆQ default)
[–]**stflush**	enable/[disable] **flush** after **write**
stop c	use c to suspend output (ˆS default)
[–]**stwrap**	disable/[enable] line shortening
susp c	use c to suspend all foreground processes (ˆZ default)
swtch c	exit to **shl** command from layer (ˆZ default)
tab$n$	set output delay after horizontal tab (**0** to **3**)
[–]**tabs**	[expand to spaces]/preserve output tabs
time c	set **TIME** value to c (used with **–icanon**)
[–]**tostop**	[do not] send SIGTTOU when background process writes to terminal
tsetcoff	xmit clock not provided
tsetcrbrg	output rec baud rate generator on EIA-232-D pin 24
tsetctbrg	output xmit baud rate generator on EIA-232-D pin 24
tsetcrset	output RC on EIA-232-D pin 24
tsetctset	output TC on EIA-232-D pin 24
vt$n$	set output delay after vertical tab (**0** or **1**)
werase c	use c to erase preceding "word"
[–]**xcase**	[do not] change case on local output
xpixels n	set horizontal window size to n pixels

(continued)

    xcibrg   use internal baud generator for xmit clock
    xcrset   use EIA-232-D pin 17 as xmit clock
    xctset   use EIA-232-D pin 15 as xmit clock
    ypixels n set vertical window size to n pixels

SU — Become Another User
% **su** [*option*] [*user* [*args*]]
Option:
    –   change environment as if user logged in

SUM — Compute File Checksum
% **sum** [*option*] *file*
Option:
    −r   use alternate checksum algorithm

SYNC — Write Unwritten Info in Memory to Disk
% **sync**

TABS — Set Terminal Tabs
% **tabs** [*taboption*] [**− T***type*] [**+m***n*]
taboption: set tabs at columns; use only 1 option
    − − *file*   first line of *file* read for tab specifier
    n1,n2,...   arbitrary ascending values (up to 40 in list);
                   if a number is preceded by **+** it is added
    −n $1*n, 2*n, ...$
    −8   standard tabs, every 8 columns (default)
    −a   10,16,36,72 (Assembler, IBM S/370)
    −a2   10,16,40,72 (alternate Assembler, IBM S/370)
    −c   8,12,16,20,55 (normal COBOL)
    −c2   6,10,14,49 (compact COBOL)
    −c3   6,10,14,18,22,26,30,34,38,42,46,50,54,
                   58,62,67 (COBOL)
    −f   7,11,15,19,23 (FORTRAN)
    −p   5,9,13,17,21,25,29,33,37,41,45,49,53,57,61
                   (PL/1)
    −s   10,55 (SNOBOL)
    −u   12,20,44 (UNIVAC 1100 Assembler)

    +m*n*   left margin, added to tab stops (**10** default)
    − T*type*   terminal type (**$TERM** default)

TAIL — Output Last Part of File
% **tail** [*options*] [*file*]
    stdin read if *file* not specified
Options:
    +n [**bcl**]   begin n units from beginning of *file*, may be
                blocks, **characters**, or **lines** (default)
    − [*n*] [**bcl**] begin n units before end of *file* (**10** default)
    −f   follow growth of *file* (don't stop at
                end of file) (can't use with **− r**)
    −r   reverse order (can't use with **-f**)

TALK — Talk to Another User
% **talk** *user* [*tty*]

Control-L will redraw the screen; exit with interrupt
character.

TAR — Tape File Archiver
% **/usr/sbin/tar** **−** [*key*] [*files*]
    stdin read if no *files* specified
Key Format: *letter* [*modifier*]

TAR, continued
Key Letters:
c	create new tape and record *files*, implies **r**
r	record *files* onto end of tape
t	tell when *files* found, all entries if no *files*
u	update tapes by adding *files* if not on tape or if modified since last written to tape
x	extract *files*, entire tape if no *files*

Key Modifiers:

#density		# is tape drive number (**0..7**), (**0** default)
	h	high (6250 bpi)
	l	low (800 bpi)
	h	medium (1600 bpi) (default)
b *n*		*n* is blocking factor (**1** default, **20** max)
f *arch*		*arch* is the file to be used for input/output to archives (if − then **stdin** read or **stdout** written
l		complain if all file links not found
L		follow symbolic links
m		update file modification times
o		set user and group ID of extracted files to user running **tar**
v		verbose mode
w		wait for confirmation after reporting filename (**y** causes action to be performed)

Δ **TBL** — Table Formatter for **n/troff**
% **tbl** [*options*] [*files*]
    stdin read if no *files* specified
Options:
− TX	Force use of only full vertical line movements

TEE — Copy **stdin** to **stdout** and Files
% **tee** [*options*] [*files*]
Options:
− a	append to *files* instead of overwriting
− i	ignore interrupts

TELNET — Connect to Remote Using TELNET Protocol
% **telnet** [*host* [*port*]]
Commands:
? [*cmd*]		help with *cmd* if no *cmd*, prints help summary
close		close all open TELNET sessions and exit
display [*args*]		display specified **set** and **toggle** values (all values default)
mode *type*		go to specified mode if available
	character	character-at-a-time mode
	line	line mode
open *host* [*port*]		open connection to host
quit		same as **close**
send *args*		send special character sequences to remote
	?	print help menu for **send**
	ao	abort output
	ayt	are you there?
	brk	break
	ec	erase character
	el	erase line
	escape	escape

68

(continued)

TELNET, continued

	ga	go ahead
	ip	interrupt process
	nop	no operation
	synch	SYNCH (discard unread input)

set *var value*

specify value for variable

echo	toggle local echo (^E default)
eof	end-of-file character for remote
erase	erase character
escape	escape character (^] default)

flushoutput
abort output

interrupt
interrupt process

kill	erase line
quit	break

status show status

toggle *args*

toggle flags

? display local **toggle** commands

autoflush
interrupt or quit sent to remote
(stty value default)

autosynch
synch after **interrupt** or **quit**
(off default)

crmod map output <cr> to <cr><lf>
(no map default)

debug
toggle socket level debugging
(off default)

localchars
when on, recognizes local commands
which are transformed to remote
control sequences (on in line-,
off in char-mode default)

netdata
toggle display of network data in
hex (off default)

options
toggle display of internal protocol
processing (off default)

z suspend **telnet**—works in shell
with job control only

host host name or Internet address in dot notation
port port number (uses default if not specified)

TEST — Condition Evaluation

% **test** *expression*
% [*expression*]

Expressions:

n1 – **eq** *n2*	true if integers *n1* and *n2* equal
n1 – **ge** *n2*	true if integer $n1 \geq n2$
n1 – **gt** *n2*	true if integer $n1 > n2$
n1 – **le** *n2*	true if integer $n1 \leq n2$
n1 – **lt** *n2*	true if integer $n1 < n2$
n1 – **ne** *n2*	true if integers *n1* and *n2* unequal
string	true if *string* is not the null string
s1 = *s2*	true if strings *s1* and *s2* are the same

(continued)

TEST, continued

s1 **!=** *s2*	true if strings *s1* and *s2* are not the same
-b *file*	true if *file* exists and is a block special file
-c *file*	true if *file* exists and is a character special file
-d *file*	true if *file* exists and is a directory
-f *file*	true if *file* exists and is a regular file
-g *file*	true if *file* exists and has set-**GID** bit set
-k *file*	true if *file* exists and has sticky bit set
-L *file*	true if *file* exists and is a symbolic link
-n *string*	true if *string* is of non-zero length
-p *file*	true if *file* exists and is a named pipe
-r *file*	true if *file* exists and is readable
-s *file*	true if *file* exists and has a non-zero size
-t [*fd*]	true if descriptor *fd* associated with a terminal
-u *file*	true if *file* exists and has set-**UID** bit set
-w *file*	true if *file* exists and is writable
-x *file*	true if *file* exists and is executable
-z *string*	true if *string* has zero length

Expressions may be joined by

!	logical negation
-a	logical and
-o	logical or
\(*expr*\)	grouping parentheses (escaped from **shell**)

TFTP — Trivial File Transfer Program
% **tftp** [*host*]

TIME — Print a Command's Elapsed, System and User Times
% **time** *cmd*

TIMEX — Print a Command's Time and System Activity
% **timex** [*options*] *cmd*
Options:

-o	report number of blocks read and written and total characters transferred
-p[*opt*]	report process activity for *cmd* and its children

f	print **fork/exec** flag & exit status
h	print CPU time/elapsed time
k	print kcore-minutes
m	print mean core size
r	print user time/(sys+user time)
t	separate user and system CPU times

-s	report all system activity during *cmd* execution

TOUCH — Update File Access/Modification Times
% **touch** [*options*] *files*
Options:

-a	update only access time
-c	do not create non-existent *files*
-m	update only modification time
MMDDhhmm[*yy*]	new times (current time default)

TPUT — Find Out Terminal-Dependent Capabilities
% **tput** [*option*] *arg*
    reads *args* from **stdin**
Option:
    – **T***type*   specify terminal type (**$TERM** default)

Arguments:
    cap [*parameters*]
                    output sequence associated with *cap*

    cap   name of capability in **terminfo** database
    parameters parameters passed to *cap*

Common Capabilities:
    blink   turn on blinking
    bold   turn on extra-bright mode
    civis   make cursor invisible
    clear   clear screen & home cursor
    cnorm   make cursor normal
    cols   outputs number of columns on screen
    cub1   move cursor left 1 space
    cud1   move cursor down 1 line
    cup *r c*   move cursor to row *r*, column *c*
    cuu1   move cursor up 1 line
    cvvis   make cursor very visible
    dim   turn on half-bright mode
    flash   visible bell
    home   move cursor to home
    init   output terminal initialization string
    invis   turn on invisible text mode
    lines   output number of lines on screen
    longname print long name of terminal type
    reset   output the terminal's reset string
    rev   turn on reverse video
    rmso   end standout mode
    rmul   end underscore mode
    smso   start standout mode
    smul   start underscore mode

TR — Translate Characters
% **tr** [*options*] [*string1* [*string2*]]
Options:
    – **c**   complement *sting1* with 001-377 (octal)
    – **d**   delete characters in *string1* from input
    – **s**   squeeze repeated output characters in *string2*

Strings may include:
    [*a – z*]   short form for range of characters from *a* to *z*
    [*a***n*]   short form for *n* repetitions of character *a*

Δ **TROFF** — Typeset Text
% **troff** [*options*] [*files*]
    stdin read if no *files* specified
Options:
    – **a**   output ASCII approximation to **stdout**
    – **b**   report whether phototypesetter is available
    – **c***name*   prepend compacted
                    /usr/lib/macros/cmp.[dt.][nt.]*name* &
                    /usr/lib/macros/ucmp.[nt.]*name*
    – **f**   don't feed out paper and stop phototypesetter
    – **F***dir*   search *dir* for font tables
    – **i**   read **stdin** after all files
    – **k***name*   compact macros used and place in
                    [**dt.**]*name*

– **m**name	prepend macro file **/usr/lib/tmac.**name
– **n**n	number first page n
– **o**list	print only listed page numbers
– **p**n	print all characters in point size n
– **q**	invoke simultaneous input/output mode of **.rc**
– **r**an	set register a to n
– **s**n	stop every n pages (**1** default)
– **t**	output to **stdout** instead of phototypesetter
– **T**name	specify output device type
– **w**	wait until phototypesetter is not busy
– **z**	print out only output from **.tm** requests
list	comma-separated, n– m means range, – n means beginning to page n, n– means page n to end

TRUE — Return Successful Exit Status
% **true**

TRUSS — Trace System Calls and Signals
% **truss** [options] cmd
Options:

– **a**	show arguments to each **exec()**
– **c**	count only calls, faults and signals instead of line-by-line trace
– **e**	show environment strings passed on **exec()**
– **f**	follow all children created by **fork()**
– **i**	don't display interruptible sleeping calls
– **m**[!]fault	machine faults to trace or exclude (**–mall –m!fltpage** default)
– **o** ofile	write output to ofile (**stderr** default)
– **p**	interpret cmd as list of process IDs
– **r**[!]fd	show buffer contents for reads on specified file descriptors (**–r!all** default)
– **s**[!]signal	signals to trace or exclude (**–sall** default)
– **t**[!]call	system calls to trace or exclude (**– tall** default)
– **v**[!]call	show structures on system calls (**– v!all** default)
– **w**[!]fd	show buffer contents for writes on specified file descriptors (**– w!all** default)
– **x**[!]call	show call arguments in raw form (**– x!all** default)

Notes: ! is used to negate the meaning of an option; **all** can be used to specify all members of a list. All lists are comma-delimited.

cmd　　　UNIX command to execute or PID list with – **p** option

Θ **TSORT** — Topological Sort
% **tsort** [file]
　stdin read if no file specified

TTY — Display Terminal's Name
% tty [*option*]
Options:
–l	print synchronous line number if connected
–s	silent mode, no output: successful exit status if **stdin** is a terminal

U3B — Return True Exit Status if Using a 3B2O
% u3b

U3B2 — Return True Exit Status if Using a 3B2
% u3b2

U3B5 — Return True Exit Status if Using a 3B5
% u3b5

UMASK — Set File Creation Mask
% umask [*option*]
    if *option* not specified, current mask printed
Option:
ugo	3-digit octal code specifying denied file access permissions. Each of the *ugo* digits formed of *read* (04), *write* (02), & *execute* (01) permissions for the classifications of *user*, *group*, & *others*.

UNAME — Print System Name
% uname [*options*]
Options:
–a	print all information
–m	print hardware name
–n	print node name
–p	print host's processor type
–r	print operating system release
–s	print operating system name (default)
–v	print version number of operating system

Θ **UNGET** — Void SCCS File Get
% unget [*options*] *files*
    names of SCCS files read from **stdin** if *files* is –
Options:
–n	do not remove file retrieved with **get**
–r*sid*	specify SCCS ID of version to void
–s	suppress output of SCCS ID on **stdout**

UNIQ — Report Repeated Lines
% uniq [*options*] [*input* [*output*]]
    stdin read if *input* and *output* not specified
    stdout written if *output* not specified
Options:
–*n*	skip *n* fields from start of line
+*n*	skip *n* characters from start of field
–c	output unique lines, count repeated ones
–d	only one copy of repeated lines output
–u	only unique lines in *input* output (default also outputs one occurrence of repeated lines)

UNITS — Interactive Measurement Units Conversion
% units

UNPACK — Unpack Compressed File (See **PACK**)
% **unpack** *files*.**z**
  unpack from *files*.**z** to *files*

USAGE — Command Usage Examples
% **usage** [*options*] [*command*]
  menu displayed if no arguments given
Options:
  −**d**   print command description
  −**e**   print command examples
  −**o**   print command options

  command   a UNIX command to print info for

UUCP — UNIX to UNIX Copy
% **uucp** [*options*] *files dest*
Options:
  −**c**   use *files* directly when transferring (default)
  −**C**   copy *files* to spool directory before transmit
  −**d**   make all required directories (default)
  −**e***sys*   execute the **uucp** command on remote system
  −**f**   do not make intermediate directories
  −**g***grade*   set job priority
  −**j**   print job ID on **stdout**
  −**m**   send mail to requester when complete
  −**n***user*   notify *user* on remote system when *file* sent
  −**r**   queue files but don't initiate transfer
  −**s***file*   report status to *file*, must be full pathname
  −**x***level*   debugging at *level*

  dest   destination consists of
                  [*sys_name*!]*pathname*
                  ˜ may be used to specify user's directory
  grade   letter or number; lower ASCII sequence
                  gives higher priority
  level   **0−9**; higher numbers give more
                  information

UUDECODE — Decode ASCII Representation of File
% **uudecode** [*encoded_file*]
  stdin read if no files specified

encoded-file is decoded and resulting file is written
to name specified in *encoded-file*

UUENCODE — Encode Binary File into ASCII
% **uuencode** [*source_file*] *file_label*
  stdin read if file not specified

source_file   name of file to encode
file_label   file name to use when decoding

UUGLIST — Print Service Grade List
% **uuglist** [*option*]
Option:
  −**u**   print grades allowed by user

UULOG — **uucp** Log Maintainer (See **UUCP**)
% **uulog** [*options*] [*sys*]
Options:
  −*n*   **tail** −*n* of log
  −**f***sys*   **tail** −**f** of file transfer log for system *sys*
  −**s***sys*   print information on work with system *sys*

(continued)

    –u_user_   print information on work for _user_
    –x   look in **uuxqt** log file for system

sys is system name; can be specified in either place

UUNAME — List **uucp** Names of Systems (See **UUCP**)
% **uuname** [_options_]
Options:
    –c   print **cu** names of systems
    –l   print local system name
    –v   print additional info about system

UUPICK — Accept/Reject **uuto** Files (See **UUTO**)
% **uupick** [_option_]
Option:
    –s_sys_   search only PUBDIR for files from system _sys_

UUSTAT — **uucp** Status and Job Control
% **uustat** [_options_]
General Status/Cancel Options:
    –a   output all jobs in queue
    –j   list total number of jobs displayed
    –k_ID_   kill **uucp** job identifier _ID_
    –m   report accessibility status for all systems
    –m_sys_   report accessibility status of _sys_ (_sys_=**all**
                       for status of all systems)
    –M_sys_   like **–m**, but include time last status obtained
                       and time of last successful transfer to _sys_
    –n   suppress **stdout**, show **stderr**
    –o_n_   status of all requests older than _n_ hours
    –O   report status using octal codes
    –p   execute **ps –flp** for all PIDs in lock files
    –q   report job numbers, control files & time oldest
                       & youngest files queued for each system
    –r_n_   set last modified time of job _n_ to current time
    –y_n_   status of all requests younger than _n_ hours

Remote Performance Options:
    –c   display average queue time,
                       not average transfer rate
    –d_n_   use _n_ minutes in calculations (**60** default)
    –t_sys_   report transfer rate or queue time for _sys_

Remote System/User Status Options:
    –s_sys_   status of requests logged with _sys_
    –S_flgs_   report job state
                    flgs are:
                    c   completed
                    i   interrupted
                    q   queued
                    r   running
    –u_user_   status of requests from _user_

All options except **–s** and **–u** are mutually exclusive.

UUTO — Public UNIX-to-UNIX File Copy
% **uuto** [_options_] _files dest_
Options:
    –m   mail when copy is completed
    –p   copy _files_ to spool directory before transmit

UUX — Remote UNIX Command Execution
% **uux** [*option*] *cmd*
Option:

–	**uux**'s **stdin** becomes *cmd*'s **stdin**
– **a***user*	user ID is *user* (user running **uux** default)
– **b**	return input if exit status is non-zero
– **c**	don't copy file to spool directory (default)
– **C**	file to spool directory
– **g***grade*	set job priority
– **j**	print job ID
– **m***file*	report transfer status to *file*, mail when complete if no *file* specified
– **n**	don't notify user
– **p**	same as –
– **r**	queue files but don't initiate transfer
– **s***file*	report status to *file*, must be full pathname
– **x***level*	debugging at *level*
– **z**	notify user if successful
grade	letter or number; lower ASCII sequence gives higher priority
level	**0–9**; higher numbers give more information

VACATION — Automatically Respond to Mail
% **vacation** [*options*]
Options:

– **d**	append date to log file
– **F** *userid*	forward to *userid* if unable to save
– **l** *log*	log of originators who have seen message (**$HOME/.maillog** default)
– **m** *mfile*	save messages in *mfile* (**$HOME/.mailfile** default)
– **M** *msgfile*	canned message file (**/usr/share/lib/mail/std_vac_msg** default)

Use **mail – F** " " to turn off vacation capability.

Θ **VAL** — Validate SCCS Files
% **val** [*options*] *files*
    command lines read from **stdin** if *files* is –
Options:

– **m***text*	*text* is compared with value of **%M%** keyword
– **r***sid*	specify SCCS ID of version
– **s**	suppress **stdout**
– **y***text*	*text* is compared with value of **%Y%** keyword

VAX — Return True Exit Status if VAX–11/750 or 780
% **vax**

Θ **VC** — Version Control
% **vc** [*options*] [*control_statements*]
Options:

– **a**	replace keywords in all text lines
– **c***c*	change control char to *c* (: default)
– **s**	don't print warning messages
– **t**	ignore chars from beginning of line to first tab

Control Statements:

:asg *keyword=value*	assign *value* to *keyowrd*
:ctl *c*	change control char to *c*
:dcl *keywords*	declare *keyowrds*; comma-separated

VC, continued

:err *message*
>> print *message* on **stderr**; halt execution;
>> return exit code 1

:if *condition* <input lines>
>> **:end**
>> if *condition* true copy input lines to **stdout**
>> Operators:
>> | | |
>> |---|---|
>> | = | equal |
>> | != | not equal |
>> | & | and |
>> | I (pipe) | or |
>> | > | greater than; unsigned integers only |
>> | < | less than, unsigned integers only |
>> | () | logical groupings |
>> | **not** | invert value of condition |

:msg *message*
>> print *message* on **stderr**

:off turn keyword replacement off

:on turn keyword replacement on

::text remove leading control chars; substitute values for keywords

keywords ≤ 9 alphanumerics, no blanks or spaces
values   ASCII or numeric strings

VEDIT — VI For Beginners (see VI)
% **vedit** [*options*] [*files*]
Options:
See **vi** for options

VI — Screen Editor
% **vi** [*options*] [*files*]
Options:

+*pos*		position file at *pos* (end of file default)
−c	*cmd*	execute *cmd* in editor
−C		work with encrypted file (simulate C cmd)
−l		set up for editing LISP programs
−L		list filenames of files saved in crash
−r	*file*	retrieve last saved version of *file* after system or editor crash (list of all saved files default)
−R		read-only mode (same as **view**)
−t	*tag*	edit file containing *tag* and position editor at its definition
−w*n*		set default window size to *n*
−x		create or edit encrypted file
pos		any editor command not containing a space

VIEW — Read-Only Screen Editor
% **view** [*options*] [*files*]
Options:

+*pos*		position file at *pos* (end of file default)
−c	*cmd*	execute *cmd* in editor
−C		work with encrypted file (simulate C cmd)
−l		set up for editing LISP programs
−L		list filenames of files saved in crash
−r	*file*	retrieve last saved version of *file* after system or editor crash (list of all saved files default)
−t	*tag*	edit file containing *tag* and position editor at its definition

(continued)

VIEW, continued

-wn	set default window size to n
-x	create or edit encrypted file
pos	any editor command not containing a space

VPR — Spooler for Versatec Printer
% **vpr** [options] [files]
    stdin read if no files specified
Options:

-c	print from a copy of the files
-ffile	use file as dummy filename for reporting completion to user
-m	send mail when printing complete
-n	don't mail after printing done (default)
-p [**-e** file]	use **vplot** to output files by **graph**
	-e output scan converted raster file
-r	remove files after spooling

WAIT — Wait for Background Processes to Complete
% **wait** [id]
    id   process ID to wait for; default is all

WALL — Broadcast to All Users
% **/etc/wall** [file]
    message read from **stdin** if no file specified

WC — Count Lines, Words and Characters
% **wc** [options] [files]
    stdin read if no files specified
Options:

-c	output byte/character counts
-l	output line counts
-w	output word counts

Θ **WHAT** — Print SCCS Identifying Information (%**Z**% Value)
% **what** [option] files
Option:

-s	print only first occurrence of pattern

WHO — Who is on the System
% **who** [options] [file] [**am i**]
Options:

-a	turn all options on
-b	list time and date of last reboot
-d	list expired processes not respawned by **init**
-H	print column headings
-l	list lines available for **login**
-n n	display n users/line
-p	list active processes spawned by **init**
-q	quick; only names and user count
-r	list info on run-level of **init** process
-s	list current users' name, line and time logged-in (default)
-t	show last time **date** changed clock
-T	list info on state of terminal
-u	long list of info on logged in users
file	read instead of **/var/adm/utmp** for login information
am i	outputs who you are logged in as

WHOIS — Internet Name Directory Service
% **whois** [*option*] *name*
Option:
  −h *host*   search on specified host

name can be a user name or handle
.*name* matches user name only
!*name* matches handle only
**name* matches group or organization
name... matches anything beginning with *name*

WRITE — Write to Another User
% **write** *user* [*tty*]

XARGS — Construct Argument List and Execute
% **xargs** [*options*] [*cmd* [*initial_args*]]
Options:
  −eeof   set end of file string (underscore default)
  −ireplace   cmd executed with occurrences of
          replace in **stdin** replaced by *initial_args*
  −ln   cmd executed for each n lines of arguments
  −nn   cmd executed with up to n arguments
  −p   prompt user whether each cmd invocation
          is to be executed (**y** confirms execution)
  −sn   max size of any argument list is n characters
  −t   trace; executed cmds output to **stderr**
  −x   stop if any argument list greater
          than size n characters

Θ **YACC** — Yet Another Compiler Compiler
% **yacc** [*options*] file
Options:
  −d   **#defines** for token names and codes to
          y.tab.h
  −l   no **#line** constructs in **y.tab.c**
  −Qn   suppress tool ID information (default)
  −Qy   put tool ID information in output
  −t   include debugging code in **y.tab.c**
  −v   parse tables and grammar reports to
          y.output
  −V   print version information

NAWK/AWK

Abbreviations
ex   arithmetic or string expression
re   regular expression (See Page 88)
str   string
var   awk variable

Program Format
- Program consists of one or more lines like the following:

    pattern { *statements* }

    Function definitions have the form:

    function *name*(*var1*,. . .) { *statement* }
- Statements are executed for each pattern that matches current record
- Missing pattern matches all records
- Missing statement prints current record
- Comments start with a # and continue to the end of the line
- Positions and offsets start at 1 (not 0)

Variables
- Variable names start with a letter
- Names can contain letters, digits, _
- Array Reference: *var* [*ex*]
- Built-In Variables

ARGC	command-line argument count
ARGV	command-line arguments (array)
FILENAME	name of current input file
FNR	record number in current input file
FS	input field separator (blank and tab default)
NF	number of fields in current record
NR	number of current record
OFMT	output numeric format (%.6g default)
OFS	output field separator (blank default)
ORS	output record separator (newline default)
RLENGTH	string length from last re match
RS	input record separator (blank means blank line)
RSTART	beginning position of string in last re match
SUBSEP	subscript separator (\034 default)
$0	complete input record
$i	field *i* of input record

- Type Conversion

    Automatic between numeric and string

    Force to string: *ex* " "

    Force to numeric: *ex* + **0**

Patterns

BEGIN	matches before first record
END	matches after last record
/re /	matches if regular expression matches current record
match	matches if match expression is true
relation	matches if relation is true

- Patterns may be combined with logical operators
- Range of patterns specified as: *pattern1*,*pattern2*
- ( ) can be used to group patterns

Match Expressions

ex ~ /*re*/	true if *re* matches expression
ex !~ /*re*/	true if *re* doesn't match expression

Regular Expressions

c	any character except special chars / ( ) * . | + ? [^ $ matches itself
c	matches special character *c*
nnn	matches char with ASCII value *nnn* octal
.	matches any single character except newline
[*list*]	matches any character in *list*; *list* is one or more single chars or ranges specified with –
[^*list*]	matches any char not in *list*
^	anchors pattern match to start of string
$	anchors pattern match to end of string

- Combining Regular Expressions:

(*re1*)(*re2*)	matches concatenated *re*'s
re *	matches 0 or more *re*'s
re +	matches 1 or more *re*'s
re ?	matches 0 or 1 *re*
re1|*re2*	matches *re1* or *re2*
(*re*)	matches *re*

( ) are optional; they ensure precedence.

Expressions

- Arithmetic and String Operators:

ex + *ex*	add
ex – *ex*	subtract
ex * *ex*	multiply
ex / *ex*	divide
ex % *ex*	modulus
+ *ex*	unary plus
– *ex*	unary minus
var ++	post-increment
var – –	post-decrement
++*var*	pre-increment
– –*var*	pre-decrement
(*ex*)	grouping
ex1 *ex2*	concatenation
ex1 ? *ex2* : *ex3*	conditional

- Assignment Operators:

var = *ex*	assign to *var*
var += *ex*	add to *var*
var –= *ex*	subtract from *var*
var *= *ex*	multiply by *var*
var /= *ex*	divide by *var*
var %= *ex*	*var* modulo *ex*
var ^= *ex*	*var* to the *ex* power

- Relational Operators:

ex1 < *ex2*	less than
ex1 <= *ex2*	less than or equal
ex1 == *ex2*	equal
ex1 != *ex2*	not equal
ex1 >= *ex2*	greater than or equal
ex1 > *ex2*	greater than

NAWK/AWK, continued
Expressions, continued
* Logical Operators (can use with patterns):
ex1 **&&** *ex2*	and
ex1 **||** *ex2*	or
!*ex*	not

* Examples of Constants:
5678	integer format
5.43E+21	exponential format
987.654	decimal format
"this is it"	string

Operator Precedence
* Highest to Lowest
* Parenthesis can be used to reorder precedence
* **:?** and **^** are right associative; all others are left

$	(field)
++ --	
^	
+ – !	(unary)
*** / %**	
+ =	
string concatenation	
< <= > >= != ==	
in	(array membership)
&&	
||	
:?	
= += –= *= /= %= ^=	

Statements
* Statements end with **;** , **}** or <newline>

* Flow of Control:
break	exit enclosing **while** or **for**
continue	next iteration of **while** or **for**
delete *var*[*ex*]	remove element *ex* from array *var*
do *stmt* **while** *expr*	
exit[*ex*]	exit awk; return *ex*
for ([*ex1*];[*ex2*];[*ex3*]) *stmt*	
for (*var* **in** *array*) *stmt*	
	step through array
if (*ex*) *stmt1* [**else** *stmt2*]	
next	skip to next record
return [*ex*]	
while (*ex*) *stmt* repeat *stmt* while *ex* is true	
{ *stmt* . . . }	grouping

* Arithmetic Functions:
atan2(*ex1,ex2***)**	arctan of *ex1/ex2* in radians
cos(*ex***)**	cosine of *ex* radians
exp [(*ex*)]	exponential function (base **e**)
int(*ex***)**	integer part of *ex*
log(*ex***)**	natural log of *ex*
rand()	pseudo-random number on interval (0,1)
sin(*ex***)**	sine of *ex* radians
sqrt(*ex***)**	square root of *ex*
srand([*ex*]**)**	new seed for rand
	(default = current time)

- String Functions:

  If *ex* is optional the default is **$0**.
  In **sub** & **gsub**, **&** in *str1* is replaced by substring matched by *re*.

  gsub(*re,str1*[*,str2*])   globally substitute *str1* for *re* in *str2*
  (returns number of substitutions)

  index(*str1*, *str2*)   position of *str2* in *str1* (returns offset if found; 0 otherwise)

  length [(*ex*)]   length of string

  sub(*re,str1*[*,str2*])   substitute *str1* for *re* in *str2*

  split (*str,a* [*,fs*])   split *str* into array *a* using separator *fs* (**FS** default)

  sprintf (*fmt* [*,ex* . . .]) returns expressions formatted by *fmt*

  substr (*str,pos* [*, len*])
  substring (*len* defaults to remainder of *str*)

- Input/Output Functions:

  close(*ex*)   close file or pipe

  getline   set **$0** to next input record; set **NF**, **NR**, **FNR**

  getline <*file*   set **$0** to next record of file; set **NF**

  getline *var*   set *var* to next input record; set **NR**, **FNR**

  getline *var* <*file*
  set *var* to next record of *file* (returns 0 on EOF, -1 on error, 1 otherwise)

  print ([*ex1* [*,ex2* . . .]])
  print expressions (**$0** if no expressions)

  printf (*fmt*[*,ex1* . . .])
  print using C-like format

- Printing functions can be redirected with **>** and **>>**
- ( ) are optional on **print** and **printf**
- one statement may be piped using **|** "*cmd* "

- Print Format Conversions:

  %c   character
  %d   decimal
  %e   exponential notation
  %f   floating point
  %g   shorter of **%e** or **%f**
  %o   unsigned octal
  %s   string
  %x   unsigned hexadecimal
  %%   print %

  Modifiers:

  –   left justify expression
  width   pad field to *width* chars (leading 0 means pad with 0s)
  .prec   max string width or number of decimal digits

System V SHELL

General
Each command consists of a series of *words* separated by *whitespace*.

Whitespace consists of one or more spaces and/or tab characters. In addition, words are terminated by any of the following characters:
; & ( ) | ^ < > newline space tab

A *list* – one or more *pipelines* and *lists* can be separated by ;, **&**, **&&**, || and optionally terminated by ; or **&**.

A pipeline consists of a command or multiple commands connected by a pipe (|).

Other variables used in the System V Shell:
n – an integer
name – the name of a shell variable
oct – an octal number
pat – explained in conjunction with the **case** command.
word – a generic argument; a word. Quoting may be necessary if it contains special characters.

Control Commands
case *word* **in** [*pat1*[|*pat2*]...)*list*;;]...**esac**
> execute *list* associated with *pat* that matches *word*
> *pat* is a word that may contain the wildcard characters *****, **?** and **[ ]**
> | is used to indicate an **or** condition

for *name* [**in** *words*] **do** *list* **done**
> sequentially assign each *word* to *name* and execute *list*
> if **in** *words* is missing, use positional parameters

funct ( ) { *list*; }
> define function *funct*; body is *list*

if *list1* **then** *list2* [**elif** *list3* **then** *list4*]...[**else** *list5*] **fi**
> if executing *list1* returns successful exit status, execute *list2* else ...

(*list*) execute *list* in a sub-shell

{*list*;} list is executed in current shell

while *list1* **do** *list2* **done**
> execute *list1*; if last command in *list1* had a successful exit status, execute *list2* followed by *list1*; repeat until last command in *list1* returns an unsuccessful exit status

until *list1* **do** *list2* **done**
> like **while** but negate termination test

Parameters
$_n_	use positional parameter *n*
$*	all positional parameters
$@	all positional parameters
"$*"	equivalent to "$1 $2 ..."
"$@"	equivalent to "$1" "$2" ...
$#	number of positional parameters
$–	options to shell or by **set**
$?	value returned by last command
$$	process number of current shell
$!	process number of last background cmd
$CDPATH	search path for **cd** command

Parameters, continued

$HOME	home directory for **cd** command
$IFS	field separators (**space**, **tab**, **newline**)
$LANG	name of current locale
$MAIL	name of a mail file, if any
$MAILCHECK	
	check for mail every *n* seconds (**600** default)
$MAILPATH	
	filenames to check for new mail (: separator; *filename* may be followed by %*message*)
$PATH	command search path
$PS1	primary prompt string (**$**)
$PS2	secondary prompt string (>)
$SHACCT	accounting file for user shell procedures
$SHELL	name of default shell
name = word	
	set *name* to specified word
$*name*	reference to shell variable *name*
${*name***}**	use braces to delimit shell variable name
${*name – word***}**	
	use parameter *name* if set, else use *word*
${*name = word***}**	
	as above but set *name* to *word* also
${*name ? word***}**	
	use *name* if set, else print *word* and exit
${*name + word***}**	
	use *word* if *name* set, else use nothing

Note: using *name* : instead of *name* checks if *name* is set and non-NULL; using *name* checks only if *name* is set.

Input/Output

All of these operators may be preceded by an optional file descriptor. Defaults are shown in parentheses.

<*file*	use *file* as **stdin** (fd0)
>*file*	use *file* as **stdout** (fd1)
>>*file*	like > but append to *file* if it exists
<&*n*	duplicate input file descriptor from *n* (**stdin**)
>&*n*	duplicate output file descriptor from *n* (**stdout**)
<&–	close **stdin**
>&–	close **stdout**
<<*word*	use following lines as **stdin** until line with *word* encountered

If any of *word* is quoted, no additional processing is done on input by shell. Otherwise:
- parameter & command substitution occurs
- escaped newlines are ignored
- a \ must be used to quote \, $, '

<<– *word*	as above with leading tabs ignored

Special Characters

|	pipe – connects two commands
;	command separator
&	run process in background; default **stdin** from **/dev/null**
&&	run following command only if previous command completed successfully
||	run following command only if previous command failed
'	enclosed string to be taken literally

Special Characters, continued

"	enclosed string to have parameter and command substitution only
`	in-line command execution
\	ignore special meaning of following character
?	match single character in filename
*	match 0 or more characters in filename
[*chars*]	match any of *chars* (pair separated by a – matches a range)
[!*chars*]	match any except *chars*

Built-In Commands – simple commands executed by sh

#	start of comment; terminated by a newline
. *file*	read and execute commands from *file*
:	null command; returns 0 exit status
[	see **test**
break [*n*]	exit from enclosing **for** or **while** loop
cd [*file*]	change current directory to *file*
continue [*n*]	do next iteration of enclosing **for** or **while**
echo [*words*]	echo *words*
eval [*words*]	evaluate *words* and execute result
exec [*words*]	execute *words* in place of shell
exit [*n*]	exit with return value *n*
export [*names*]	export *names* to environment of commands
getopts	parse parameters and options
hash [– **r**] [*files*]	remember locations of *files*; with no *files* shows hash info; – **r** forgets all remembered locations
newgrp [*words*]	same as **exec newgrp** *words*
pwd	print working directory name
read *names*	read **stdin** and assign to *names*
readonly [*names*]	mark *names* read-only; print list if no *names*
return [*n*]	exit with return value *n*; with no *n* return status of last command
set [– *options*] [*words*]	set flags (**aefhkntuvx**– are valid) (see **sh** command); *words* set positional parameters
set [+*options*] [*words*]	unset flags (see **sh** in Commands section)
shift [*n*]	rename positional parameters; $*n*+1=$*n* ... (*n* defaults to 1)
test	evaluate conditional expressions (see **test** in Commands section)
times	print accumulated process times
trap [*word*][*sigs*]	execute *word* if signal in *sigs* received; no *word* or *sigs* – print traps; no *word* – reset *sigs* to entry defaults; *word* is null string – ignore *sigs*; *sigs* is **0** – execute *word* on exit from shell
type*files*	show how shell would interpret each *file*

Built-In Commands, continued

> **ulimit** [*type*] [*options*] [*limit*]
>> *type* (default is both):
>>> – **H** hard limit
>>> – **S** soft limit
>>
>> *options*:
>>> – **a** all (display only)
>>> – **c** core file size (512-byte blocks)
>>> – **d** "k" of data segment
>>> – **f** file size (512-byte blocks)
>>> – **n** maximum field descriptors +1
>>> – **s** "k" of stack segment
>>> – **t** cpu seconds
>>> – **v** "k" of virtual memory

> **umask** [*oct*]
>> set file creation permissions mask
>> to complement octal *oct*
>> (see **chmod** for details of *oct*)

> **unset** [*names*]
>> unset variables or functions *names*

> **wait** [*n*] wait for process *n* ; if no *n*, wait for all
>> children

Job Control

If invoked as **jsh** the following additional commands
are available.

> **bg** [*jobid*] resume execution in background
> **fg** [*jobid*] resume execution in foreground
>> or moves background job to foreground
>
> **jobs** [*option*] [*jobid*]
>> report status of stopped/background jobs
>>> – **l** report PGID and current dir of jobs
>>> – **p** report only PGID of jobs
>
> **jobs** [–**x**] *command* [*args*]
>> replace *jobid* in *command* or *args* with
>> PGID and execute *command* passing *args*
>
> **kill** [– *signal*] *jobid*
>> built-in version of kill for job control
>
> **stop** *jobid*
>> stop specified background jobs
>
> **suspend** suspend execution of current shell
> **wait** [*jobid*]
>> wait that uses *jobid*; if **%***jobid*
>> missing it behaves like regular wait

jobid, the job identifier for a job, defaults to the current
job, and can specified using the following list:

> % current job
> %*n* job number
> + current job
> – previous job
> **?***str* job uniquely identified by *str*
> **PID** process ID
> *pref* job whose command line begins with *pref*

REGULAR EXPRESSIONS

Regular expressions are used in many UNIX utilities: **vi**, **ed**, **sed**, **grep**, **egrep**, and **awk**.

Regular expression characters overlap with shell metacharacters. You can use single quotes to "insulate" them from shell interpretation.

Summary of Regular Expressions In Decreasing Precedence	
c	if non-special char, matches itself
c	turn off special meaning of *c*
^	beginning of line
$	end of line
.	any single character
[...]	any one character in ... or range
[^...]	any one character not in ... or range
n	what the n'th \\(...\\) matched (grep only)
r*	zero or more occurrences of *r*
r+	one or more occurrences of *r* (egrep only)
r?	zero or one occurrences of *r* (egrep only)
*r1*l*r2*	*r1* or *r2* (egrep only)
\\(*r*\\)	tagged regular expression only (grep only)
(*r*)	regular expression (egrep only)

NOTES

NOTES

NOTES

NOTES